THE SMART
TAKE FROM
THE STRONG

The Basketball Philosophy of Pete Carril

Pete Carril

with Dan White

UNIVERSITY OF NEBRASKA PRESS
LINCOLN AND LONDON

First Nebraska paperback printing: 2004
Book design by Jeanette Olender

Library of Congress Cataloging-in-Publication Data
Carril, Pete.
The smart take from the strong: the basketball philosophy of Pete
Carril / Pete Carril with Dan White.
p. cm.
Originally published: New York: Simon & Schuster, c1997.
ISBN 0-8032-6448-8 (pbk.: alk. paper)
1. Basketball—Coaching.   2. Basketball—Philosophy.   3. Carril,
Pete.   4. Basketball coaches—United States—Biography.
I. White, Dan.   II. Title.
GV885.3.C37   2004
796.323'07'7—dc22   2004005374

To my high school coach

   Joseph Preletz

and my college coach

   Bill Van Breda Kolff,

and my best friend

   Rocco Calvo.

Two coaches and a friend

without whom I never would

have had my time at bat.

CONTENTS

THE SMART
TAKE FROM
THE STRONG

INTRODUCTION BY BOB KNIGHT

Having played against and watched Pete Carril's teams for almost thirty years, I have great admiration for Pete as a coach and a teacher, and equally great respect for him as a person. He is an extremely honest man with great integrity. Pete has always been straightforward in everything he has done.

My first contact with Pete Carril was not as a coach, but as a player. This was in the 1960s, when we were both working at basketball camps in the Pocono Mountains and would wind up, over the noon hour or late at night, playing in three-on-three games. It had been some time since either of us had played college basketball, but my first impression of Pete was that he must have been an extremely smart player. I saw in him in those three-on-three games the same tremendous understanding of how the game should be played and the great competitiveness that I've come to admire enormously in Pete as a coach.

His teams play with a soundness at both ends of the floor that is seen in very few teams. They are always conscious of making it as difficult as possible for you to score; they are relentless in preventing easy baskets. On the offensive end, they make it very difficult for you to defend against them because of their ball-handling ability, movement, and patience in waiting for the right opportunity to score. From the positioning and footwork at the point where the guard picks up through every phase of defensive play to the final block-out when a shot is taken, Princeton players have always exhibited the results of Pete's teaching and understanding of the game. The same is true from the time the ball goes into the hands of a Princeton player until a shot is taken on the offensive end of the court. There is no coach who has done a better job of teaching his players how to read the defense—what it is doing, or going to do, and how to react to it—than Pete has during all the time he has been at Princeton.

I have always tried to tell my own players that the two key ingredients in success in basketball are playing hard and playing intelligently. No one has gotten more out of these two characteristics than Pete has with his teams. They absolutely epitomize playing the game as hard and as intelligently as it can be played. Pete has always provided his players with what I think is one of the best testing grounds in all of college basketball, that is, an extremely difficult nonconference schedule. His teams have played anyone, anywhere, and always provided the opponent with the ultimate test at both the offensive and defensive ends of the floor. Just as Pete has been a great teacher of the skills of the game and the result has been the intelligent play of his teams, he has also been a great motivator of players in getting them to play to the full extent of their abilities. Pete is an outstanding combination of teaching ability and motivational skill. Pete Carril has been a tremendous asset to the game of basketball and a great credit to it. I feel honored to have been asked to comment about this man who has given the game of basketball far, far more than he has taken away from it. I can think of no better compliment that a basketball coach could ever receive than to be told, "You know, your teams play a little bit like Pete Carril's Princeton teams used to play."

Who Takes from Whom?

My father came from the province of León in Castile, Spain and worked for thirty-nine years in the open-hearth for the Bethlehem Steel Company. Every day, before he left for work, he would remind my sister and me how important it was to be smart. "In this life," he would say, "the big, strong guys are always taking from the smaller, weaker guys but . . . the smart take from the strong." Then, as he was going out the door, he would point his finger at his head and say, "Use El Coco." That has been a theme of my coaching, and so when I began to think about writing down some of my thoughts and observations about basketball, I wanted the title to reflect that. An athlete who is fundamentally sound and plays intelligently and hard will generally come out on top.

The Nature of a Coach

You take a bird. Every bird wants to fly; that's his nature, his whole life. Well, every coach wants to win. And so do I. You play basketball with integrity and to win.

To win? Not just to play your best? No. What other reason besides winning is there for sports in the first place? When you strive to win, you find out what kind of person you are going to be in later life. Sure, when one guy is five times as good as another, that won't come out, but when you are nearly equal it does. Whenever two players or teams of equal ability play, the one with the greater courage and intelligence will win. If a player will work out his limitations on his own, practice long hours, if he will do all these things, he will win.

Winning brings out the best in people who are good, the worst in people who are not. Losing does not build character. If the players want to lose, here is all they have to do: drink, smoke, lie, be lazy. I guarantee you the team will lose every time and you will have a team of characters.

In America today, coaches are judged by whether they win or lose and not by how well they teach. So winning is what you worry about most—winning and all the factors that affect the chances of winning: the character of the players, recruiting, admissions, financial aid, academic pressures, luck. I define success as having a chance to win every game. It's my job to give my players the chance to have their character, their drive to win, determine the outcome. And then the quality of your teaching—your own character—comes out.

A lot of coaches act like their main job is to keep from getting fired. They practice good behavior, have strong handshakes, wear the right clothing, use hair dryers, and so on. They present themselves with the quintessence of sartorial splendor. But if they don't know what they're doing, they might as well be naked. As for me, I have an image, too. My clothing, often ridiculed, is not Armani style, but it's good, it doesn't cost much, and it's never prevented me from doing what I know I have to do. I have always tried to be on the outside what I am on the inside. What you see is what you get.

Pick Your General

Some people like General Patton. I like General Grant. A Spartan way of life is not for everybody.

The Only Difference

A very important part of my life is teaching. At some big-time basketball universities, the emphasis is on recruiting: "Let's get a coach who can bring in talent." For me, the basic thing has to be teaching. I was reading in the newspaper once about a professor who was retiring and the kind of teacher he had been: very demanding, always insisted on best effort, a little cantankerous. I thought, "Hey, they're talking about me, except that I yell and swear."

When you teach basketball, it has its technical parts and its life parts. It has to be that way, because it's played by humans. You'd be surprised how many people forget that. It's the human who gets tired, who stops trying, who gets mad at his girlfriend, or his father, or his coach. And it's the human who doesn't care enough to do every single time what he has to do to win. When you draw X's and O's on a board, you can change them around easily and predictably, but put a human being in there and the symbols won't predict what will happen. That changes the essence of all sports.

In 1990 we played Arkansas in the first round of the NCAA, and with a minute and a half to go, we were up by one point. To win a game like that you have to play a perfect game, or if you make a mistake you have to be lucky and get away with it. Our strategy for that game was not to play on the high side of Oliver Miller, one of their centers, who with another of their big men was shooting better than 50 percent. They were so broad-shouldered that when other teams tried fronting or high-siding them, they couldn't get around them and Miller and his buddy were getting easy layups. So our tactic was to get behind him, between him and the basket, so that he couldn't drive, and instead had to shoot the ball over us. Well, he wasn't used to that and didn't shoot well, so our strategy seemed to be working for us as the game went on. We had trailed by as much as 14 in the game, but we'd closed the gap and were winning by a single point near the end when all of a sudden my guy decides to try to get around Miller and intercept a pass to him in the pivot—in other words, to try to do what no one else had been able to do very well all season. And like all the others, he couldn't get around Miller. So he doesn't get the steal, Miller lays the ball up and we lose. Here's a kid who had played exactly the way we needed to play Miller the entire game with great effect, so what possessed him to change that? Something human. What you must realize is that you cannot coach without factoring in the human equation.

When you're coaching, you cannot help teaching the parts that apply to life. When your guy sets a screen to free one of his teammates for a shot, and a defender comes running at him full speed and he knows he is liable to get hurt, does he have enough courage to set the screen and take the hit, to finish the job? That is the life part. Patrick Ewing of the New York Knicks earns—how much? Five or six million a year? And he will step in front of a man driving and take the charge, risking injury and his career, while another player earning just as much will not. The guy without that life part moves out of the way prior to contact. Why do some players get tired and give up and why do some players get tired and keep on going? This is what I mean when I talk about a life part. I don't know that you can teach it, but you must stress it. Stressing it is how you find out who has it. And sometimes those who don't seem to have it really do, but the circumstances of their life before you got them have been such they've never had to demonstrate it. You have to help them change. That's what education is: changing behavior.

What Turns Me On

Some guys, they look at an automobile and their eyes light up like you can't believe. They slam the doors, they check the tires, they do everything. When they go to wash that car, it is unbelievable what they do. Some guys take a look at a girl, and they watch her all the way down the street. Unbelievable. I take a look at a basketball player who's got some innocence in his face, with eyes that are telling me he wants to be good and wants me to help him—that turns me on.

Behaving Wisely

Great philosophers of education have said there are two things important in learning. Both begin with a definition of the words *to know*. One is learning facts, data—information. The other is knowing how to behave intelligently. They are both important, but one is more desirable than the other.

That is what discipline means: *behaving wisely*. It has nothing to do with saying "Yes, sir," "No, sir."

Some guys know about things, but their actions are not wise or mature. Coaching is helping guys behave and act wisely—to do the smart thing. Any jackass can teach a Shuffle Offense or a zone defense, but the quality that makes the exceptional coach like Vince Lombardi is the ability to get the player to do what he does not want to, and do it well.

How We Learn

Three factors influence your behavior. One is the way you think about something. Two is that what you see is affected by the way you think. And three is that what you see affects what you do. If you think you must get the ball inside to win, then you will see something different from another coach who doesn't believe that's what he has to do to win. And because you believe that, you will try to push the ball inside and you might insist on it even though it's so unreasonable it might result in missed shots, not catching the ball, or committing violations—but you think you have to do that to win, and so it influences what you do. Some coaches don't like the three-point shot and so they see offense differently and don't teach the three-pointer, whereas other coaches like Rick Pitino and I like three-point shooting and we teach it.

John Dewey, the American philosopher and educator, said you learn through experimentation and practice, which I interpret to mean you learn by doing the exact thing that you are trying to learn, i.e., through direct experience. Ask any lawyer and he'll tell you that you learn more about law on your first case than you ever did in law school, or ask the French teacher and he'll say that you learn more actually teaching French than from having studied it.

Nowadays, someone will take that "exact thing" and break it down into its components, into a whole bunch of steps, with each step leading back toward the whole. The theory is that by learning to do each step, then advancing to the next, at some point you can put them together and you have learned the whole. I believe you have to *teach* the whole. Take the three or four basic dribble moves: the crossover, the reverse pivot, an inside hand change, and the stop-and-go dribble. The best way to teach those moves is to work on each one of them in its entirety, as opposed to ball-handling drills like dribble tag, or wearing blinders, or a whole bunch of other silly drills where you might get good at that drill—at tag or dribbling with blinders—but when you're done, you still can't do the crossover or the reverse pivot. Teach the specific skill.

The Only Objective Standard

Overemphasizing winning is bad, but singling out winning as the most important thing you can do is good, and you should do everything you can to prepare so you can win. Winning is the only objective measure for a team; all the rest is subjective. A typical squad has fifteen guys, and at least seven think they should be playing and two more think they aren't playing because you the coach don't like the way they look at you, or the length of their hair, or their father, or their uncle; one guy thinks he's working harder than the next; one guy says he feels discriminated against; and so on. Fifteen players and it's chaos, but if you're winning, it's harder for the malcontent, for the overly ambitious parent, whoever, to argue that the team is suffering because his son isn't playing. Winning solves a lot of problems. I once had a guy come to see me —we were in first place, 11-3 on the season, and he wanted to know why we weren't playing him. He tells me he is working harder than his roommate, who was starting for us. So I told him to go tell his roommate what he had told me. Naturally he didn't, and he didn't stay on the team. What kind of guy would do that to his roommate?

Never Say Never

Two words to avoid in teaching are "always" and "never." There is nothing that happens a certain way 100 percent of the time. Another way of saying that is a coach does not want to be right more than 85 percent of the time.

Flexibility is key. Coaches and players who recognize that will not make the mistake of doing something the same way all the time. If you always do something one way, it will kill you. Shooting layups, for example: We shoot layups every day for eight minutes, and I insist that my players develop different ways of laying the ball up. Nothing in basketball is done 100 percent the same way every time. Conditions change, and if you shoot layups the same way every time, you may not be able to adjust. A good example of this was our game against Georgetown in 1989. Our player Bobby Scrabis drove the baseline and Alonzo Mourning came down to block the shot. If Scrabis had taken the shot on the side of the basket from which he started, the shot would have been blocked. Instead, Scrabis went under the basket and made a reverse layup, which we practice every day.

There is a tendency today to stuff the ball exclusively and not practice layups. What happens if you find someone in your way and you can't stuff the ball and instead try a layup, but you haven't practiced layups? You won't make the layup. You have to be able to adjust to changing conditions.

The Coach's Job

A coach's job is to put his team where it can function effectively and win. That's more true with older kids whose habits are well established than with younger kids, where the coach has to work on teaching them the fundamentals and how to develop the right habits. His other main job is to make each player better than the man he is playing against.

You try to put a player in a situation where those things he does well can occur. For example, he might not dribble very well, so you have him cut or set screens, and so on. I had a player named Billy Kapler (Class of '73) who could not catch the ball very well when you threw it to him, but when he got a rebound you could not knock the ball out of his hands with a sledgehammer. How do you account for that? You can't, but you have to recognize that. He could rebound and he could defend, so we had him set an awful lot of picks for other guys, whereas if we had had him shooting the ball, or catching it . . .

You might have a team that is not very fast, and can't get shots for themselves. Their shots get blocked, they stumble

25

around, they make violations. You have to work out some way for them to get free, so you set more screens, create more movement, make it possible for each player to help the other more. You make the defense move, and that makes it possible for slow guys to play. We had another big man named Howard Levy ('85), and at the time we liked to have our center come out and shoot from the top. Howie didn't make too many of those, so we changed the way we played to more of an inside game. The defenses started packing it in against us, giving us outside shots that were closer and easier—but frankly, they didn't go in either. Sometimes you have the solution, but it still doesn't work.

Knowing What to Coach

It's in the best interests of a coach to make sure he is not spending three hours a day practicing things that don't happen very much. If you watch what your players are doing when they play, they'll show you what to teach them—that's an important principle in coaching. When a coach picks a style of play, that style cannot be his; it has to come from what his players indicate they can do and can't do.

When I first came to Princeton, we had fast teams and averaged close to 80 points a game—I like to remind people who criticized us recently for playing a deliberate style of offense, or a slowdown game, of that little bit of history. Our later offense wasn't slow; it was judicious. As the players got slower afoot here, they dictated to me that it was time to change our style of play. If a coach has a fast team and he wants to play a control game because that's his style, he'll have a revolution on his hands—the players will naturally want to run. On the other hand, if you have a slow team and it's your style to run and the other team beats you down the court, you had better change that, too. Your team will dictate the things you can teach them—and you find out by watching them carefully.

The Kind of Coach I Am

I want things to go right all the time every day.

Winning is in the details. Maybe other coaches would be satisfied with a guy driving through the middle and passing the ball to an open teammate. But not me. I also expect such a pass to be delivered to the shooter's shooting hand so that the ball can be caught and released quickly and efficiently. We work on those details by the hour.

The coach has to make sure that he is watching, and that he corrects every mistake, and doesn't take any shortcuts—doesn't say, "Well, I'll let it go this time and catch it next time." I have never believed in the theory that sometimes what you do not notice is better. I have always been alert to what has to be taught and watched and corrected. When the game starts, it is rare that my team doesn't know or have some experience with what is going on. One year, we went into the season not having prepared against a 2-3 zone or a 1-2-2 zone because I thought we would be good enough shooters to keep teams from playing that way against us, but we were not. Not that I took anything for granted, but our preparation just had not been completed. So after that, as I evaluated my teams, I always took into account the fact that my evaluations might be wrong, too.

What to Emphasize

Whatever you emphasize and to the degree that you do, you get better at it. Let's say you develop a defense that prevents easy, unrestricted movement of the ball. You'll be better at that than somebody else who does not emphasize it, up to the level of your talent.

It's results that count, and they should determine your principles. How does that player make that pass, how does that shot get in there—so on and so forth? The point is that the pass does get made, and the shot does go in. It is a mistake we all make as coaches to think that there is only one way of doing something. There is not. Whatever works works.

Make Sure They Are All Listening

When you explain a point to player X, the other players should listen so that they know about that point as well. There's a tendency for players to believe that because the coach is talking to someone else, they don't have to listen. If they're all listening, the coach won't have to repeat the same thing to the guys who weren't involved, and everyone will know what player X is doing on a particular play, and therefore what his options are. Each player has to have an idea of what every one of his teammates is doing. Not only does it save time when you are teaching something, but it enhances the effectiveness of what you are trying to do.

I Can Teach a Guy Basics

One of the things I'm grateful for about my coaching career is that I started teaching guys to play in tenth grade. I call that starting from scratch. I taught basics, right from the beginning, and as a result I learned how to teach a player to dribble, to pass, and shoot. Sometimes it was so hard. I used to say that this kid couldn't dribble a ball across the street, or couldn't pass it to an open man because he couldn't throw apples in the ocean. Now that's the bottom.

My first job was as a jayvee coach at Easton High School. I had just been discharged from the Army, I'd played basketball at Lafayette in Easton, Pa., I had a teacher's certification and something of a name locally, so it seemed like a natural thing for me. The first day of practice, the team manager asked me to turn on the lights in the gym because he thought I was the janitor. The kid's name was John Curley, and he now heads up Gannett Newspapers, and his younger brother, Tom, is head of *USA Today*. I had eight players my first year and I spent a lot of time teaching fundamentals. I remember one player named Charlie Ross who came down from the varsity because he needed a jump shot. I worked with him for four games and he moved back to the varsity and went on to become an all-time great at Lafayette. I had to teach him and the others how to pivot, hang in the air, where to hold the ball, and when to let go of it—we worked on all that stuff.

29

Then, I went to Reading, from a great football town to a great basketball town, and it was more basics. Even at the college level, I always spent a good half hour every day on basics. And one thing I noticed: Sometimes in an effort to shorten our practices, we cut out the basics. If we did that for a long period of time, the guys began to slip.

And now I'm teaching basics in the pros. I'm working with one pro now who is making the transition from center—from playing with his back to the basket— to a number three or outside player. He is an excellent dribbler and passer, and is very fast, but he has to work on his shooting. I think he's holding the ball too high, slinging it with his hand, not using his whole arm. His elbow is too straight and he can't get his hand under the ball. When you go to change a player, you have to know he is not having success where he is. And you have to see some little thing about the way he handles the ball, some quickness, some agility, something that makes you think you can make the conversion. Because the basics remain the key to success on every level of the game, and you can teach them. And you have to.

The Truth About Fast Players

Wherever fast players go, they always get there faster than slower players.

■ ■ ■

Teaching Versus Coaching

There is a difference between teaching and coaching. When you are instructing your team about the actual game, you are teaching them, transmitting knowledge and information to them. There are guys who don't teach their players anything or much of anything, but who go around and recruit the best players and they win—they're coaches but not teachers. Other guys may not get the best players, but they still go about trying to teach them things; they are coaches but also teachers. The best situation of all is to be able to attract the best talent *and* be a teacher; that is what distinguishes coaches like Mike Krzyzewski at Duke, Bobby Knight at Indiana, Rick Pitino at Kentucky, Dean Smith at North Carolina —although it is unfair to single them out because there are another 150 like them whose schools are not as prominent so they can't attract the talent. You can't control everything.

One thing I do know about my coaching, which I have always done and could not do any other way, is that I prepared my team to win every game they played regardless of where they played and whom they played. That was a definite—you could count on that. There have been at least fifty games that no one thought we could win: UCLA, Georgetown, North Carolina, Duke, Arkansas, Kentucky, Nevada-Las Vegas, Syracuse, and so on.

I always recognized the severity of the difficulty of the challenge we faced. What good is it being Spanish if you cannot tilt at windmills? But I don't think there is anything inherent in my Spanish temperament that caused me to think I could win. I think it was growing up in South Bethlehem, where I had a close family situation, good friends, terrific teachers. I think the war (WWII) also had an influence. You saw all your older neighborhood friends, your idols, go off to war, a lot of them local athletes you had tried to emulate. We sat in the school cafeteria with the newspaper, the *Allentown Morning Call* and the New York *Daily News,* and followed the progress of the war, the maps with arrows showing troop movements, and you would always know that forty or fifty of your friends were there. When they came back, it made you grow up fast just to be around them. That was very important to me. The result of all this—if you believe as I read somewhere that your personality is the sum total of all your experiences—you learned to try as hard as you could no matter what, and you never spent time thinking you could not win. All your friends thought the same way.

Preparing to play a national power was difficult at times. You always had to look at the things you saw you could do well and not give up on those. In 1977 we played Kentucky in the first round of the NCAAs and lost. The week before, my assistant coach Tony Relvas, who played at Easton, made us work harder running things in practice against him than we had to against Kentucky, though we still could not overcome their superior talent. But we tried to create conditions in practice that were as hard as or harder than any that my players would meet in a game; if we succeeded, that would help my players see that they could do some things well and be successful, so they went into the game believing that they had a chance to win and nothing that happened in the game was a surprise. We were getting ready to play Holy Cross in 1975, and they had a terrific press. Gary Walters ('67) was my assistant then, and he threw up such a hard press against us in practice that week that we had trouble just getting the ball inbounds. I told the players not to worry, that it would be easier against Holy Cross, and it was—we scored 84 points and ran right through their press. The point is, you try to do those things well that matter and you work hard to do them right. If you have good work habits, you don't have to worry about who you play, or where, or when, or whatever. You have your work habits to fall back on.

You have to be a little careful: I remember late in the 1969 season, we went to Cornell undefeated, having already clinched the Ivy title. I said to my players before the game, "Fellows, we have had to win a lot of games, but this is a game we do not have to win. We would like to win, end up undefeated in the league, but we don't really have to win. The pressure is off." So I was walking out of the locker room and the players were huddled over in the corner, and they were making bets about how long it would take for that speech to hit the wastebasket. Forty seconds into the game, we're behind and playing badly and I'm hollering like crazy. That's when I looked down my bench and all my guys were laughing like hell. We won, 74–64. I guess it mattered.

What to Be Good At

As a player, you want to be good at those things that happen a lot—that cannot be overstated. What happens a lot? You dribble, you pass, and you shoot—you want to be good at those skills. That is one of those things in basketball and sports and life that go without saying, but ought to be said regularly. If what you are doing—what you are good at—doesn't happen that often, then there's no real benefit to being good at it. A wise player understands all that. A younger player might not.

I see a lot of guys working on stuffing the ball. I recognize the value of that, but when it is done at the expense of other things—like shooting layups different ways—it's wrong. I remember a player who used to do a lot of stretching before practice; that's important, but he would overdo it. He would lie down on the floor, put his feet on the wall, push hard, bend and stretch his legs, do all kinds of things to loosen up. In the meantime, the captain Mike Brennan ('94) would come out and start shooting. By the time the guy stretching was done, Brennan would have shot two hundred or more times Which is going to help you become a more productive player? When Bobby Slaughter ('78) first came to campus, he was interested in trying to touch the rim with his elbow. By the time he graduated, he had become one of the best to ever play here. He realized that touching the rim did not mean a thing; what mattered is that he discovered he could dribble and defend very well and he could see people everywhere on the court.

A coach must try to instill the ethos that simplicity in an effective, functional way is what counts, not style. Michael Jordan can run like a deer and jump out of the gym; those are the two skills everyone notices, but they totally obscure the fact that he is fundamentally sound. He is good at all the things that happen a lot. So was Larry Bird, and so was Magic Johnson and so are all the players who are great because they are so skilled in those areas of the game.

■ ■ ■

What I Look for in a Player

I had a friend named Les Yellin. We became very close friends while I was at Princeton. He coached basketball at St. Francis College in Brooklyn—had been a fine player himself. When we talked about players and what qualities we value, he had a way of summarizing the main virtues in the form of acronyms that I liked. He referred to them as "IQ," "EQ," and "RQ." IQ means what it always means—the function of intelligence. Behaving intelligently covers the whole realm of knowing what to do. A smart player will not take a shot he knows he can't make. He will know not to stop a guy from shooting who can't shoot. He will know things about himself that enhance the way he plays.

EQ is energy quotient, which means having the energy to work at what you're doing. "Fatigue makes cowards of us all" —Vince Lombardi, the great coach of the Green Bay Packers, gets credit for saying that. If you stop to think about it, when most people get tired, what happens? They just throw in the sponge. They would like to do this, or do that, or perform at a high level, but they are too tired to do it. There is a Spanish saying that goes like this: "When the legs go, the heart and the head follow quickly behind." When your EQ is good, you practice harder, play the game harder, and when it looks as though you cannot move anymore, you find a way to move some more.

RQ stands for responsibility quotient. You know what to do, you have the energy or EQ, and now you have to know that whatever it is, it must be done. You are likely to do well those things you want to do. But there are also those things you may not want to do but have to do, and have to do well. My philosophy is always to do what I have to do, and if it turns out that it's also something I want to do, that is just that much more gravy. When a kid growing up sees what he has to do and does it, that is his RQ. You must immerse yourself in the selfish development of your own skills, and then put those skills to use in the context of playing with four other guys so that you aren't working against yourself and are behaving toward them in a responsible way, and they to you. These, again, are personal character traits that determine so much of what happens on a basketball court.

Modus Operandi

Ginger Rogers once complained to Fred Astaire that he forced them to practice so much that she just hurt all over. "Why do we have to work so hard?" she asked, and he replied, "To make things easy."

I tell my guys that if they work hard every day, then they don't have to worry about game plans, or where they play, or whom they play, or about rankings and so on. The quality of their work habits can overcome anything: praise, criticism, good or bad coaching. They have their daily behavior to fall back on. Their "modus operandi" comes out. I try to tell them we are all creatures of habit and have to get into some kind of groove where our habits are good ones. Good habits are hard to break and so are bad ones. I try to get them to understand: If they learn to do things right, or well, that gets to be the way they do things, and whatever happens, that isn't going to change.

Workers get the most out of themselves; when a body has limited talent, it has to muster all its resources of character to overcome this shortcoming. If you think you are working hard, you can work harder. If you think you are doing enough, there is more that you can do. No one really ever exhausts his full potential. Winning takes character and intelligence. It is the most important thing you can do because it's a reaffirmation of your character.

Have you ever watched violinist Itzhak Perlman when he plays? His facial expressions, the intensity of his feeling for every note . . . if you want to be as good at what you do as violinist Itzhak Perlman is at what he does, then do what he does: work, work, work.

A Body with No Talent

I had a guy here, Billy Sickler, who was the epitome of excellent work habits. He was my captain in the 1970–71 season. I remember one game where we beat Maryland 75–67, and after the game the press was asking me about this kid's performance. He was a small forward, 6' 3", 175 pounds, who also played guard when needed, though he definitely was not a guard. He had a terrific game, scoring 22 points, 16 in the second half. He shot 12 of 13 from the free throw line. He was simply great, especially for a body with limited talent. He wasn't a great dribbler, a great passer, or a great shooter—but he sure could do the job when we needed it. It was amazing the way he worked so hard.

By no talent, I mean in terms of quality talent. Billy did not have the talents of a lot of other players; when I first saw how slow he was, I tried to figure out how he could ever play. So what he did for us that night was all the more to his credit.

He had the courage of a lion and dogged determination. I said then that I would be a coach a long time before I saw another kid like him. He brought the ball up for us in that game without losing it, and he took that good kid they had, Rod Horst, and he stopped him cold, and then he took their captain, Tom Milroy, and held him to one basket.

Well, I said all this to the press and I got a hard time afterward for what I'd said about his not having any talent. He became our best defensive player that year. He never stopped guarding his man and he always took the toughest opponent. I always pushed him harder than the others because I knew he needed to work extra hard to get the playing time he wanted. I always admired him for his work habits and his courage, and while I pushed him, I never yelled at him, or almost never. In fact, that got to be a problem: I began to notice that all the other players were getting mad because I never yelled at him. One day I decided I had better fix that, so I went out there and start yelling at him: "Sickler, you keep messing up like that, you're going to find your rear end on the plank." He looked at me all startled, like "I didn't do anything." This went on for a couple of days in a row until I saw that everyone else was happy, and then I stopped. I finally explained it to him when he graduated.

That summer, I spent a few days recruiting on Long Island with Billy. First thing I would do in the morning is visit two or three schools and talk to the guidance counselors. About one o'clock, Billy and I would go down to Jones Beach with a basket of chicken and some beer with a friend of his from Dartmouth, Joe Cook, and sit down and talk about basketball. We'd go swimming, and they were trying to teach me how to surf. One day, I got out too far and my arms and legs were getting tired. I yelled, "Billy, you may have to come out here and help me come in." He didn't say anything for a while, and then he yelled back, "I don't know if I want to." I love that story.

We keep in touch, and when I changed from a man-to-man to a zone defense, I got a check from him for a contribution to our basketball fund and a note saying that as soon as I switched back to the man-to-man, he would double the amount.

You Cannot Hide on the Court

I can check the level of your honesty and commitment by the quality of your effort on the court. You cannot separate sports from your life, no matter how hard you try. Your personality shows up on the court: greed, indifference, whatever, it all shows up. You cannot hide it. It's possible to be a phony on the court and still be successful if you have talent by relying on talent instead of hard work. You think you're skilled enough to take shortcuts, to cheat on the effort it requires. But you cannot hide it.

When I say talent I mean having the skills that when used properly insure success. The more talent you have, the greater your margin for error, for gambling, for risk. You can violate some general principles if you have talent, because the mistake you make will not kill you. For example, take Brian Taylor ('73). One of the fundamental principles of defense is that you defend a cutter by staying on the ball side of the cut. Brian was fast enough that he could trail the cutter by a step, and when the passer threw him the ball thinking he was open, Brian could step in front and intercept. Another example might be someone who has a knack for rebounds and doesn't spend as much time boxing out. He goes after the ball and gets it.

Without talent, then, developing precision and trying to do things 100 percent correctly will reduce the number of mistakes and, therefore, the number of failures. Suppose a guy is wide open on the left side of the court, and you have the ball on the right side. Normally you require two passes to hit the open man in this situation. If the first pass is thrown off course a little and the guy catching it has to bend over, and then he throws it even worse, by the time the pass gets to the open man he'll be covered. Whereas if the passes had been properly thrown, getting the ball over there without any problem . . . every little thing counts.

Overcoming Certain Obstacles

A good mind has never handicapped a player.

Emulate the Great

Opposing coaches and players always said you could not tell what my team was doing. That's because we tried to teach our guys the skills and style of the great players. The great players are the ones who can dribble, pass, and shoot. Michael Jordan, above all, is the super player of all time because he can do everything. He captivates the entire country, actually the world, with his play. But with the millions of kids who are playing basketball, are you telling me that there is only one player like him? I say a lot of the reason that there are not more is attributable to what's being done at the lower levels of coaching. Kids are not learning the basic skills of the game because it takes too much time to teach them, because coaches and players alike want immediate results, and because the number of coaches who can and will teach young kids is declining. You can take a bunch of ten-, eleven-, twelve-, thirteen-, and fourteen-year-old kids, and after working hard with them you'll have a bigger headache than any migraine. It is hard to teach things that take time to learn.

One other thing regarding Michael Jordan: He is on television all the time. He only has a few more years to play. I would say that the 500,000 kids who are his size and have ability should start imitating him; it is not a facetious statement to say you want to be like Mike. For that matter, think of Bob Cousy, Elgin Baylor, Larry Bird, Bill Russell, Bill Walton, Kareem Abdul-Jabbar, Magic Johnson—so many guys to imitate that it's a mystery to me why we don't have another 300 good basketball players in this country. And by imitation, I don't mean wearing his jersey.

Kids should try to imitate a top player who does things that they're likely to do as they get older and more mature. Don't try to do those things they do that you cannot do. When you see someone stuff the ball, don't start trying to stuff it if you don't have that kind of jumping ability; if you see a slick guard who makes one-handed passes, don't start doing that just because it looks neat, since it can lead to bad habits. I find that most college players today are totally ignorant of what they need to make the jump to the pros: What they need are excellent fundamentals. What the hell are they watching when they watch a pro game on TV? What are they seeing?

41

The Three Basics

If a guy cannot pass, the ball stops moving. If he cannot shoot, he will always be open. If he cannot dribble, he cuts his value to the team by one third. Furthermore, if he cannot dribble, the defense will attack him.

Dribbling

The high school coach who does not make his players learn and practice dribbling should be arrested. Dribbling is one of those things that are easier said than done. I believe there is limited teaching of dribbling today in part because twenty, thirty years ago, there was an excess of dribbling, and this dearth of emphasis on the teaching of it is still a reaction to that.

Dribbling has to be developed when the player is young. The player has to know why, when, and where to dribble, and how much. The player who cannot dribble is restricted, no matter how tall, no matter what his role on the team is, and that includes big men who are often coached as youngsters just to shoot and rebound. My teams at Princeton warmed up every day by dribbling the ball. We also played a lot of one-on-one where we required the player to dribble with his weak hand. We told him he could not shoot unless he dribbled first.

The object of dribbling is to control the ball with either hand to go where you want to go. A good dribbler can dribble anywhere. I like the hand on top of the ball, and I like the ball in front on the dribble, not on the player's side. Most of the time, if you dribble with the ball on your side, you tend to carry the ball instead. Carrying the ball, or palming it, is prevalent now in the NBA; no one seems to stop it, and I think we're going to see more of it in college.

I have never seen a great low dribbler. All the great dribblers like Bob Cousy, Walt Frazier, Oscar Robertson, and Isiah Thomas were high dribblers. When you dribble low, it compresses your body too much, and you can't move. Of course, in a crowd, if you dribble too high, you'll lose the ball. With the ball at your waist, you can move quickly. When you enter a crowd, you had better bend over a bit to protect the ball.

You want to keep your head up and dribble without looking at the ball, which is also easier said than done. If you're looking at it, you can't see the defender, or anyone else on the court. With Cousy, the ball was there somewhere but he never looked at it.

Your basic dribble moves should include a crossover dribble —you have the ball in the right hand and you move it across to the left and vice versa. The dribbler kicks off with his right foot if he is going left. His head is always up. You use the crossover to penetrate the defense, to start something, to get a shot off. Archie Clark of the Lakers was a great practitioner of the crossover—no one could ever stop it.

There is also a spin move, or "the Pearl Move," because Earl "the Pearl" Monroe was the greatest practitioner of it. This is another way of describing the reverse pivot—you move one way, then reverse direction with an inside hand change. The ball never comes across the body, it stays on the same side. Knowing how to do the spin move is only part of having a good spin move; the other part is knowing when to use it and when not to use it. I see some players who don't know when to use it and they spin right into the defender instead of away from him. You have to try not to work so hard on one dribble move that it becomes the only one you have.

There is a whole bunch of dribbling drills, but my complaint about some of them is that they aren't connected to the actual skill and situation in a game. No drill is any good unless it's used in some form in the game. There is no transfer of learning; you learn the crossover move or the spin move by doing them. When you put somebody in front of the dribbler everything changes, so you have to practice dribbling against a defender if you want to become a good dribbler.

You have to play a lot to become a great dribbler and if you don't play much, there's no way to make up for it. Sometimes, I get kids at my camp whose parents have told them to carry a basketball everywhere, even sleep with it, as if having their hands on the ball all the time molds their hands so they'll be better dribblers. That's crazy. At my basketball camp, I always ask the kids if they know how to dribble. Everyone always raises his hand and says he does and they do, in the sense that everyone knows the rules about dribbling. But I might find one kid out of 200 who can actually dribble and move where he wants to with control of the ball. Anybody can know the facts about something, but knowing how to do it is what's crucial.

If you want to become a better dribbler, dribble. Dribble on a court, with a man guarding you. The dribbler has to learn how to set up the man guarding him. The defender doesn't have eyes in the back of his head and doesn't know where the dribbler is going. You can move him in one direction or another, away from where you eventually want to go. The defender will only know what you're going to do if you're limited in your dribbling skill and experience. If you're a great dribbler like John Stockton of the Utah Jazz, who has all the dribble moves, the defender has no idea what you're going to do with the ball. When you reach that level, then you are a dribbler.

Some of it is intuitive. The rest is practice and experience. Gary Walters ('67), whom I coached at Reading and who then became one of Princeton's greatest guards of all time during the Bill Bradley era and is now the director of athletics there, had the smallest hands you ever saw. But he was one of the best dribblers I ever saw. Nobody ever took the ball away from him, or from Armond Hill ('76). They had natural ability and worked hard at becoming great dribblers.

You would think that at the highest level of play—the NBA —everybody could dribble. But they can't. It's one of those skills we are not paying enough attention to. And one reason for the decline of good dribbling is what I describe as the increased specialization of basketball: a team assigns the major responsibility for dribbling to a play-making guard, who is basically the team dribbler. After him, the rest are suspect.

I think basketball today is overly specialized. Instead of forwards and guards and centers, you have numbers that refer to a specific role or function that the player performs. The number one man is the point guard and his job is to bring the ball up and start the offense. Then you have the two man, a shooting guard whose main function is to shoot. The three man is supposed to be the best all-around athlete, meaning he can dribble, pass, and shoot. The four man is usually dis- tinguished by the fact he plays with his back to the basket but is generally smaller than the five man, the center. He is responsible for rebounding and low pivot activity.

Each is trained in the particular function of his role, but they're so specialized that you can't always get them to do other things, or they never develop the skill. Coaches don't take the time when the players are young to teach all of them all the basic skills; a coach might see a big man start to dribble and holler at him: "Hey, don't dribble; give the ball to the guard to dribble. Your job is to get rebounds and shots in close." Or you see a point guard who can dribble the air right out of the ball, or a shooting guard who can't do anything but shoot. These are the kind of players you love to play against.

The players themselves, when they're young, are impatient, and they don't want to take the time to develop other skills if they see right away that what pleases their coach, what produces immediate results like winning and success, is performing one particular function. So they don't learn the skills, and it becomes hard for them to adjust and improve: for a point guard to give up the ball, because that is contrary to what he's been taught growing up and that is what he knows how to do; or for the shooting guard to play the other end of the court, because his role has always been to score.

I have my centers do the same dribbling drills as guards and forwards. I get criticized for making centers and forwards learn to dribble, but think of the number of times when the centers make the final play on a three-on-two fast break. You want a center who can dribble. A forward or center who can dribble can play anywhere. When Bill Walton was forced to the bench with his injuries, he was in the process of revolutionizing the way all centers play because of his mobility and his dribbling ability. Look at Magic Johnson, 6' 9"—a big man who is an impeccable dribbler. Imagine some coach trying to prohibit him from dribbling when he was a kid. And look at the Chicago Bulls—every one of them is at least a decent dribbler, and it's why they can play the way they do.

To me the trend toward systems and numbers means there isn't enough teaching going on with younger kids. Coaches are looking to win the quickest way they can, and so they fit their players into these assigned, specialized roles. Even in the high schools you hear talk about sending the four man in the hole, and the three man setting a screen for five. Every offense seems to follow the numbers now. But I still have guards and forwards, and a center. And I still try to teach them all how to pass, dribble, and shoot. And, may I say, it is very, very hard.

Pass to Play

People told my players that if they wanted to go to Princeton, they had to be able to pass to play. That was essentially correct. Passing was the single greatest attribute of my teams over the years. I loved to have passers as well as shooters, because they set up the shots that anybody can make. I love to see all my players involved in passing.

A passer who can see people open is the same guy who sees where and when to screen, avoids picks, helps on defense—in other words, he can see. The passer is the same guy who knows where weaknesses are, where the drives are, and where everybody on the floor is. He uses that knowledge to move the ball. That is why passing was so important for us. To score, you gotta move the ball. We pass to move the defense, and every pass counts. Some passes result in points, some get things started, and there's the pass before the pass that starts something. When you start your offense with a pass, the next pass becomes easier, the next one after that even easier, etc. If you start your offense with a bad pass, the next pass is worse, and then you finally lose the ball.

What I also love about passing is how much it helps to build team morale. Passing takes the tension out of a game: the tension of whether I'm going to get the ball and whether the other players have enough confidence in me that they'll throw it to me. Passing makes everybody feel a part of the game, a part of the team.

There are two basic elements to passing. One is wanting to pass and understanding its value, that's a teachable thing. The second is the ability to see people who are open. For me that has not been teachable. All great players have been able to see a lot. That's a gift; it's in their DNA. You can make it easier for a guy who can't see, but in the end, he does not see.

I have a way of determining why a player doesn't pass: If I hear him tell the open man he is sorry he did not pass the ball to him, then I know the passer saw the open man but didn't want to pass. A passer who doesn't see his teammate when he is open never says he's sorry. How do you explain his inability to see? It's like the two students in algebra who have the same teacher and one gets a grade of 95, the other 65. Why?

It's more than just seeing the open man. A great passer sees the person he is throwing to, and also sees what *he* is going to do with the ball when he catches it. A good passer might throw a pass and then see what's going to happen, whereas a great passer might *not* throw the ball because he saw what was going to happen if he did. A great passer has a softness to his pass that makes it catchable. You can't explain that or teach it.

No single aspect of basketball does more to develop good team play than passing, and conversely nothing destroys a team faster than a shooter who never passes. When the open man doesn't get the ball because his teammate has elected to take a bad shot, or done something else contrary to the best interests of the team, it's a challenge to his sense of the right way of doing things in this game. And when he retreats up court to play defense, that has its effect.

The players have to understand the need for accuracy and creativity in a pass. If our best shooter is open at eighteen feet and one of my players throws the ball to him at his knees, that's bad. Accuracy is so critical. If you throw the ball too low to a shooter, it may help him miss the shot. The pass has to be right at the chest so he is ready to shoot. That is really, really important. I know there are great coaches who don't care where the ball is caught. I do. It's a little thing, but little things lead to little things lead to little things, which lead to wins.

Passing seems a lost art in the modern game. When I visit high school clinics or camps. I work hard to impress on the players the value of passing. Sometimes it depresses me. Seventy-five percent of the players in high school will not pass the ball to an open man. That's the influence of greed. To often, players will pass only after they cannot do something else. That is not a pass.

The two-handed chest pass is the most accurate technique for passing the ball, but it's an endangered species in today's game because so many players try to emulate the pros and throw the ball across their body with one hand. You telegraph your pass that way. I try to break my players of that habit. A player can throw a variety of chest passes: left, right, up, down, long, short, and the ball always starts from the same place. It leaves the hands quickly, it doesn't take long to release, it leaves with a lot of zip, and it's hard to intercept since its direction and velocity can be disguised. Magic Johnson could throw a chest pass half the length of the court.

No pass is a bad pass if it's unobstructed to an open man:

crosscourt passes, half-court passes, full-court, diagonal, over the top of the zone, whatever. Sure, some get swiped. But the ratio of success for us is 10–2, maybe even 15–1. I never tell my guys not to throw a particular pass because results count no matter what. Bob Cousy could throw a hook pass the length of the court—if we can complete the pass, throw it.

I had a kid, Billy Ryan ('84), who was a great passer. No one every pressed us successfully while he was here. We played Boston College in 1983 in the second round of the NCAA Tournament. BC had a good press, but they overplayed us, and we ran away from the pressure by having Billy throw half-court passes over the top of their press. He and Armond Hill were both great at finding the vulnerable spot that would defeat the pressure. He was drafted by the Nets, and they came to Princeton in the preseason to practice. Ryan was with the second unit and they were working against the press. Billy did the same thing—threw the ball upcourt and broke the press three or four times in a row. It was unbelievable. (I should add that throwing the pass is only part of it; you have to have someone who can catch it as well. We beat Notre Dame in 1977 by throwing over the top of their press to one of our guards, Billy Omeltchenko. He could both catch the ball and then do something with it, like score a layup.)

Funny thing about the BC game, we had very few turnovers in the first half, and they had twice as many, so we went in at halftime down by only one after shooting 33 percent. I told the players, "Hey, fellas, we're doing okay, we're only down by one, we're getting good shots, no way we'll shoot 33 percent next half." We shot 22 percent in the second half and lost even though we handled the press and did everything else right.

Two Kinds of Elitism

When I walk across campus on a Monday after a party and see beer cans and litter, I loathe that stuff—it is elitism at its worst. I prefer the elite of workers.

Just Shoot It

It is said that the shot makes the play. Some guys try to make a real science out of shooting; they analyze every single shot and they know all the theories. I think a lot of that is overdone. I was walking by a tennis clinic the other day and the instructor was standing there talking to a bunch of kids about the mechanics of the serve. I went by again about twenty-five minutes later and the guy was still talking. I said to myself, "Whoa, when do the kids ever get to hit the ball?" If you want to learn how to shoot a specific shot in basketball, get the mechanics straight, then go out and practice hard. Once you have the right basics, you can teach yourself how to shoot: When you shoot and it feels good, then you want to imitate that form until it becomes a habit. Try not to talk too much about shooting. Spend the time instead taking a lot of shots.

In teaching shooting, you have to recognize the little differences that exist among the players, and not force each player to shoot the same way. What works for one guy might not work for another. You don't want to keep someone from doing something he's good at just because it looks funny, or it violates some principle you think makes up good shooting. I watch a player shoot, see the kind of shots he shoots, whether he makes them, whether he makes them uncontested or contested, whatever. If he makes his shots, I don't care how ugly the shot is, I don't mess with him. If he doesn't make them, then I look at a bunch of things: where his hand and elbow are, where he releases the ball, follow-through, rotation, velocity. The shooter himself will show you what you can do to help him make his shot better.

I have a few golden rules that I follow: First be ready to shoot. That statement is often not quite understood. You must know before you catch the ball that you're open and that what should be done is that you should shoot it. You are ready. The shooting hand is under the ball, and the elbow is under your hand; that provides for good rotation. Aim for the front of the rim, which allows you to make the proper follow-through. Then, take a shot that you know you can make, because knowing when not to shoot is just as key as knowing when.

I want to see a good snap of the wrist and an accentuated follow-through, which will ensure proper rotation. All great shooters have rotation on the ball. At the risk of sounding too knowing, I have never seen any great knuckleball shooters. If the shooter has a lazy or weak wrist, the motion will be jerky, and you won't have a smooth release of the ball. Shooting is one smooth, continuous motion, from the heels to the toes right up to the fingertips.

I look to make sure the elbow is underneath the hand and not sticking out sideways. I know guys who hold the ball in front of their face, with their elbow out—it's hard to make long shots that way. And I also know guys who hold the ball way back over their head and sling it. There aren't many good shooters who shoot like that—too many moving parts. If you think of the arm as a pool stick or lever, the elbow is the fulcrum (bridge) when you shoot—the point or support on which the lever turns. If you are slinging instead of pushing, the fulcrum is probably too far away from the end of the stick and you can't control the shot. If it's too close to the end, you can't get enough power or strength.

The legs provide strength and balance in shooting, from layups to jump shots. They give you lift. If the legs are undeveloped, or tired and out of condition, you end up shooting with your arms; the further out you like to shoot, the more of a problem this becomes.

I also look at the shooter's touch on the ball: the velocity of the shot, and its trajectory. It's possible to shoot too hard, for the ball to get there too fast. A lot of young shooters do that; it feels natural and makes sense in terms of the physics of their developing muscles and bones, but it leads to bad habits. They have to meet up with a coach who corrects those bad habits before they get too far along in their careers. Young players need to imitate great shooters more than they do because the quality of shooting is going down in the country. Each year, the three-point shooting percentage gets worse in the NCAA. Three-point shooting is down at Princeton from near 50 percent to 33. Foul shooting is down, too.

I like a shot that floats softly on a 45-degree angle—that's the best trajectory, though I won't quibble about degrees. It is not traveling such a great distance, and it travels on an angle that gets it over the front of the rim. If the trajectory is flat, it won't go over the front. There are guys who shoot to the other extreme, rainbows that are so high, the shot goes eight feet or more further than in a normal trajectory. To me, there are more things that could go wrong with such a shot.

Always follow through on the shot by pointing the hand as if it were following the ball into the basket. I don't like to see guys pull their hand back; that creates a hitch, although some guys pull back because they are so darn strong. There are some shooters whose wrists are so strong that they make shots more easily from a longer distance than they do from closer in.

There are different theories on what to aim for. Some coaches say you should focus on the flight of the ball. Others say aim exclusively for the back of the rim. I won't say either is wrong, but I've noticed that when I try to look just at the back of the rim, I see the front as well, and the same thing the other way around. I tell my players to aim to get the ball over the front of the rim, because when they look at the front they're more likely to see the back, too, or the whole rim.

Try to take a high percentage shot, one that you can make. Pass the ball around, move the defense, perhaps ten, twelve, twenty passes if necessary, but get a good shot. Remember that your team is never in trouble as long as you have the ball, and bad shots when missed lead to easy fast breaks for the opposition. Let's face it: You can move the ball around all you want, move the defense, get an easy shot, then miss it—and you've done all that good work for nothing. That tells you how important shooting is.

The Simple Layup

When I talk at clinics, I say that every player should have in his repertoire something that he can use to score. It may be a layup, but whatever it is, it must be something that will contribute to successful offense. If a kid learns nothing else at basketball camp except how to shoot a layup properly, that makes it worthwhile.

In teaching the layup, some coaches disagree about whether the hand should go on top or underneath the ball. I like the hand underneath. You can control the ball better, especially when you're running full-speed, where it's hard to control the ball if your hand is on top. When a player shoots a layup on the left side of the basket, he normally would do that with his left hand, but sometimes it's better for him to shoot it right-handed because doing so puts him a half step closer to the basket, or makes him quicker getting there, which can be the difference between making the shot and getting it blocked by a chasing defender. The same holds true for a right-handed shooter on the other side of the basket. The point is, don't shoot layups the same way every time. In general, get up as high as you can, and keep your eye on the target. I tell my players to shoot different kinds of layups each day so that their shots and the movement of their legs don't become stereotyped. If you jump hard each time you practice them, you'll strengthen your legs. If you practice layups casually, you'll shoot them casually in a game.

Over the last two decades, the power layup has become a part of the game. In a power layup, the shooter drives for the basket, and when he gets in close he comes to an abrupt stop (a jump stop), gathers himself and pushes off both feet for the basket, as if he were thrusting upward, going up strong—a power layup. The ball is held parallel to the head, or sometimes behind the head. It's a good layup in the right conditions, for example, when a defender is on one side of you and you haven't completely beaten him. You go up strong—you might get fouled, or you might beat him. But I've noticed a lot lately that power layups are getting blocked from behind —somebody sneaks up on the fast break or a drive and blocks the shot. That's why I like the regular layup, the layup off one foot. There, you have extension with your body so that the ball is held out further away from the defender who's chasing from behind, and your body is between him and the ball so that if he wants the ball, he probably has to foul you. A one-foot layup gets the ball to the basket quicker.

More people seem to be shooting power layups these days. A lot of people imitate Michael Jordan, who has *the right layup for every occasion.* So many players see him shoot a power layup and then try to imitate him, but they don't understand that Jordan can do the power layup because he has great spring in his legs. For any number of reasons, not everybody can do that. Their abilities don't correspond to those of Jordan and the other great players. There are also some guys who get less power off a power layup than they do off a regular layup, and they have to know that. Jumping straight up on a power layup, they might barely get off the ground, but with the extension on a regular layup provided by their momentum from running, they might be able to stuff the shot. In summary, get the ball to the basket as fast as you can, away from the defender, using either a one-foot layup or a power layup.

You Never Tire of Making Shots

Fifty years ago, you had a guy with an outside shot, and when the defenses began to press him to take away that shot, the strategy was to try to drive by the defender to make a layup. Then as defensive strategy changed, the defender began to chase him, and at the same time another defender would leave his man and step out to block the player driving to the basket. So what was the offensive player to do: a man in front, a man chasing, and he wants to shoot? He pulled up, jumped in the air, and shot. There you have the jump shot, invented out of necessity, as a shot in between the layup and the set shot. In my first two years at Lafayette, before Bill Van Breda Kolff became my coach, we had a guy show up who was a jump-shooter, which was very rare. My coach took one look at that shot the first time he saw it and told him to stuff it up his rear. Some things take a while to get used to.

Young kids can learn to shoot a jumper by standing stationary near the top of the key, facing the basket, holding the ball, and jumping and shooting at the top of their jump. Then you add a pivot: You make him face the sideline, still holding the ball, then pivot on his inside foot, jump and shoot. Then you back him off the key toward the opposite sideline, and have him run toward the top of the key, as if he were cutting to the basket, and you pass him the ball. He catches it, pivots, and shoots. That is how a jump shot starts.

The jump-shooter must be taught to jump straight up. In that way, the body and the basket are not moving relative to one another. If the body is moving in the air, then, in a sense, the basket is moving, too, and that complicates the shot. Some coaches put a dime on the floor to make the point—I don't use that particular drill, but what they're getting at is that the jump-shooter must go up and come down on a dime. You want to be sure you don't let your body drift into the defender and disturb your shot, or cause a foul. I have seen floaters in the air—shooters who drift—who make their shots. But generally speaking, in college, you'll find that most shooters who drift are not going to make that shot. In pro ball, they drift, which makes the shots harder, but it's hard to be a pro if you can't make the hard shots. If your legs are strong, they provide the same support as you go into the arc as if your feet were on the ground. Your legs will dictate the range of your shot: how far out you can shoot, how high you can go, how much control you will have of your body.

I'm not certain about this, but there appears to be a greater margin for error if you use the backboard when you shoot from different angles. The angle of incidence equals the angle of reflection—maybe it has something to do with that. I don't know, but lots of great shooters use the backboard. A lot of coaches teach their players to bank their shots, and Johnny Wooden, UCLA's great coach for so long, taught his teams to bank their shots all the time from certain spots. I do know this: You can shoot with greater velocity, and if you have good backspin, it can go in.

It might also be that when you use the backboard, it is easier to pick out a spot to aim at. A lot of players bank their shots when they are moving quickly. It may be easier when you're moving and drifting to focus on a spot instead of the rim. You hit the spot and the trajectory does not have to be that terrific.

The most likely area from which to bank your shot is along either side of the basket, eight to twelve feet out, up to an angle of 45 degrees with the backboard. I'm not talking about layups, where a player should bank the shot as a matter of routine. I have noticed that if you're left-handed and are going to bank from the right side of the court, you need a more generous angle to shoot from. The same is true on the left side if you are right-handed.

I had no preference for whether my players should bank their shots, but what I do feel strongly about is that once you decide to bank your shots, then you should go ahead and do it all the time. Don't decide to bank it and then change and shoot it cleanly. The worst thing in shooting is to be indecisive.

It's not always clear why some players are not good foul shooters. Since a free throw is only worth one point, maybe a player or a coach chooses not to spend too much time on it. But every team knows that toward the end of a tight game, foul shooting often becomes the difference between winning and losing. I have noticed that when a player shoots too often, his own teammates don't like it too much. But if he makes every free throw, no one gets upset with him except the other team. The free throw is the only shot in basketball where it's okay to be greedy.

It may be that the shooter lacks concentration. Some guys make the sign of the cross before they shoot a foul, or bounce the ball a certain number of times, or clasp the hands of their teammates to get focused. I don't know if any of that is any good, but if you're the foul shooter and you think it works, then do it. I never said too much to my players about breathing before you shoot a foul—but you should take a deep breath and try to relax.

I had this little drill to make foul shooting competitive: I divided the players into groups. Each player shoots two fouls in a row. As a group, they must make fifteen straight, and if they miss, they drop back to zero. The drill builds some pressure—the group gets up to thirteen, fourteen in a row and someone misses, they go back to zero. I cannot honestly say the drill is a factor in how my players shot fouls; I'd done that drill for years and had some great foul shooting teams and some bad ones as well, and I was the same person. I remember getting letters from coaches asking why my team never missed foul shots. The last few years, my teams had trouble making free throws and I was the same coach, and I wasn't getting any letters.

The word "never" is one I rarely use; however, may I say you should never get tired of making shots. And you should never stop trying to make them. What you want is that when the game starts, you're taking the same shot, going right back to what you did in practice, which some guys like to think of as calling on their "muscle memory." Your muscles remember what to do because you've trained them. Such a routine also provides the mental confidence you need. If you consistently make shots in practice, what's the problem with making them in the game if it's the same shot?

The only gym rat I ever coached at Princeton was Geoff Petrie ('70) and he never got tired of trying to make shots. He was always in the gym, Sundays as well, practicing his shooting. He was a natural shooter, had a great jump shot, but was also a great all-around player. He and Brian Taylor ('72) were Princeton's most gifted pro prospects during my career. He was drafted in the first round by the Portland Trail Blazers, became Rookie of the Year, was an All-Star, and scored 51 points four times.

If you make shots in practice but not in the game, it's because you don't believe in yourself, or maybe you're taking bad shots. I've had players who lacked confidence in their shooting. Sometimes with extra practice they would start to make their shots consistently, and I would remind them that they were the same shots they were getting in the game. There have been some players who shot lousily in practice, and well in a game, and vice versa—it could be concentration. A lot of players don't like to practice. But for the most part, the guys who shot well in practice are the same guys who shoot well in a game. They have the attitude that they can always do better. Some players miss and chalk it up to "just one of those days," and there are other players who will not settle for that. They want to make every shot. They practice, practice, practice.

When you practice hard those things you do in a game, then when the game comes, you've done them and you do not get nervous. If you've made fifteen shots in a row from the same spot on the court, like Bill Bradley used to do in practice, when the game starts you'll make the same shots, so long as the coach can make sure you get the same kind of shots. Which is not always easy.

I am a devotee of long-range shooting. I loved to shoot from far out and I made some, and still do. A shot is never too far out if it goes in. If you see a shooter who can make the long shot you don't stop him from taking it. I let the shooter tell me where he should go and shoot by watching to see how many shots he makes from out there. I've had some great shooters at Princeton: Geoff Petrie, Teddy Manakas ('73), Brian Taylor, Frank Sowinski ('78), Sean Jackson ('92)—to name a few. Sowinski was thirteen for fifteen against Rutgers one year, seven for eight against Notre Dame, and guarded all the other team's big scorers as well. We called him "Molasses" because he wasn't the fastest guy around. That was a nickname we used for a lot of players at Princeton.

When you make the long shot it spreads the defense over the court and makes your slower players seem taller and faster. It extends the defense, discourages the opponents from clogging the underneath area, and gives you a better chance of playing catch-up basketball when you have to. It also makes it easier to get the ball inside. It makes it harder for the defense to double down on the low post—if they double down, the ball comes right back outside for the open shot.

Today, they're making a federal case out of the inside-outside game, and the outside-inside game where you throw the ball inside and then back outside quickly for an open shot. We'd been doing that for thirty years, but now somebody decided to coin the phrase.

Try to practice shooting on the move, running both to your right and left. You have to practice catching the ball from either direction so that your pivot becomes constant, and so that you prepare for the shot in the same manner all the time. You must be able to catch the ball fifteen to eighteen feet out and shoot instantly. The more you can shoot without dribbling, the more it sets up other things. After you're comfortable shooting instantaneously without putting the ball on the floor, then you learn to shoot with a dribble. Every shot in your repertoire should be learned first without a dribble, then, after you've perfected it, with a dribble that incorporates different moves. Taking a shot off the dribble is like creating or designing your own shot.

I've seen guys—pros, too—who practice their shooting without the ball, moving around the court, going through their repertoire in a pantomime. They'll do it days on end, trying to imagine defenders in front of them. I am 100 percent against that. You learn to shoot with the ball, and if you want to learn how to shoot a specific shot, get out and shoot it. All shooting drills should replicate game conditions and situations. You can replicate shooting off a screen: You pass the ball to a player coming off a screen and he shoots, and you do that over and over so that he gets the footwork and the feeling of doing it right. Venerable Kentucky coach Adolph Rupp spent forty minutes a day having his players shoot from spots on the floor in specific game situations.

You can tell the difference between a great shooter and a

poor shooter by the number of times he makes his shot versus the number of times he misses. That sounds overly simple, but I mention it because you'd be amazed at how many bad shooters keep shooting and missing and never notice how many times they miss. I have a motto: Bad shooters are always open. It is hard to play with a shooter who doesn't make shots.

In the end, shooting is a variable: Maybe the shooter's elbow is not straight, or he is releasing the ball over his head, or he drifts when he jumps in the air to shoot. You can correct those things, but you can only improve your shooting up to a point. Not everyone is going to be a good shooter, because not everyone has that intangible known as "touch." During my forty-three years as a coach, I worked with players who are not good shooters and they improved. One of the best examples of that was a guard, Mickey Steuerer ('76), who had a bad habit of shooting the ball from way back over his head and couldn't score consistently. We asked him to move that shot forward some. That spring, every time I came to my office he was down on the gym floor practicing that shot. The next season, he became a consistent scorer, First Team All-Ivy, and All-East. I have also worked with players who were not good shooters and didn't improve. You try to get them to a level where they are not considered "missers." When a misser shoots, the whole team thinks, "He's shooting, get back." In general, I think that shooting as a skill can be improved as long as you realize that there are limits on what you can teach.

■   ■   ■

From Close In

The dunk, or stuff shot, can be a very important shot, if when you shoot it, it isn't because you can't shoot a layup. I noticed at Princeton over the past few years an increase in the number of stuff shots, and that the stuffers were not very good layup shooters.

The dunk is important because it is hardly ever missed, and the psychology of the stuff can be intimidating. It makes everyone go crazy. The crowd loves to see a monster jam: the display of raw power and jumping ability. A guy can make a three-point shot, but it doesn't provide the same terror, the same brute force, so that even though it's worth more points, the crowd doesn't respond the same way. Opposing players should try to remember that it only counts two points and not let the noise and excitement bother them.

One thing for sure, if the slam is used to excess it will begin to mean less and less to the crowd, and eventually it will lose its excitement. You have to have the proper mix of shots. It's like the home run in baseball: The minute it starts to happen too often, it will become less interesting to the crowd, and in time to the players as well.

The hook shot is disappearing in college and high school basketball because it's an ugly-looking shot. But down close to the basket, you have to ask the question, How am I going to score? And the answer is, you do whatever it takes, ugly shot or not. There are two categories of shots: those where the player faces the basket, and those made with your back to the basket. When you play with your back to the basket, you must develop a feel for where you are. One of the principal shots in this situation is the hook. Even though the popularity of the shot is declining elsewhere, in the pros more guys are hooking now because the defense is doubling down on the man with the ball. The University of Kentucky doubles down now, and I think you'll start to see more colleges do that as well. A player who is doubled is not going to get a fade-away jump shot against a double team, but depending on where the double team comes from, the hook shot can be very effective.

When a player shoots a hook shot, be it a jump hook or straightaway hook, again, I like the hand under the ball, the shooter's body between the ball and the defender. The trajectory of the shot is harder to block given the placement of the body between the ball and the defender.

Shooting Confidence

The rule for any shot depends on the player who's shooting it and his ability to make it. If the situation calls for a shot and you are not a shooter, or you don't want to shoot, there is a good chance your tentativeness or indecision—your lack of confidence—will cause a violation. During the '96 Chicago Bulls' playoffs, I saw several players commit violations because they had lost their confidence temporarily. It was unbelievable.

Compensation for Poor Shooting

There is compensation for poor shooting if you know what your limitations are and if you're willing to work. A guy like Paul Silas who used to play for the Boston Celtics was not a good shooter, but he did so many little things. He got rebounds, he made passes, he played good defense. Bill Russell, how great was that guy? He did a hundred little things, not one by itself worth very much, but together, whoa, all the little things he did added up. He set a great pick. He blocked more layups from behind by chasing guys who appeared to have uncontested layups than any other player I have ever seen. He also made more guys miss layups because they heard him coming. These little things were hard to see, but they made all the difference.

A Limit to What You Can Teach

Here is the thing about teaching basketball: It's just like teaching a subject in school, like I did when I taught economics in high school. Six or seven kids got above a 90, then maybe fifteen got between 85 and 90, on down to six or seven who flunked. You stand in front of the class saying the same thing to everyone, and yet you have these differences in their ability to learn and to utilize the information. The same is true in basketball. Remember that when you ask yourself why it is that after you've finished explaining a play, somebody doesn't get it, or doesn't know, or doesn't see what he has to do on the court, or can't shoot or pass as well as the other guy. There is a limitation on what you can teach.

■ ■ ■

Before You Give Up . . .

You have to teach your players certain things that they will learn, or not learn, at differing rates of success. And you will have someone who seems to have a terribly difficult time understanding or perfecting what it is you want him to do. But before you give up on that individual, before you stop what it is you're trying to teach him, you have to understand that you're both going to experience a period of failure.

You may ultimately have to give up on the player. But you reduce the chances of that being the case by trying to be sure that you insist on only those things that you're pretty certain the player can improve on, whatever they might be. If you're asking him to surpass the level of his talent, that will become clear after a while. Then, when you have reached the end of the line, when you've tried everything you can think of—exhausted all the possibilities—then you try to design something that will help this player avoid having to do something that he's not good at doing.

If a coach doesn't have the patience to see a player through the process of learning to dribble with his left hand, or something similar, then he can put in a system that makes the player a role player who never has to learn to dribble with his left hand. There is a tendency today among some coaches to give up too soon. The trend toward specialization is an example of that. You don't have to ask a player to improve overall; you simply assign him a specific task in a system and that's all he has to do. His teammates will be specialists, too, each complementary of one another, but not skilled in the basic attributes of the game. The net result is that the players never get to improve overall, because they get to do only the one thing they're already good at.

When you hear the pros talking about one of their colleagues not having "a game," what they mean is he is limited in the things he can do. The following players have "a game": Michael Jordan, Scottie Pippen, Penny Hardaway, Charles Barkley, Grant Hill, and a bunch of others. They distinguish themselves by being able to do whatever is required for them to be successful. They have few limitations. Teach a guy fundamentals and he can play anywhere. Without them he cannot be anywhere near as effective.

What Losing Requires

Look at all the things you have to do to win: You have to sublimate your individual greed for the sake of the team. You have to conform to certain training rules that deny you the chance of having as much fun as your friends are having. You have to provide total mental concentration. All those require a great deal, whereas losing requires absolutely nothing.

Whom Does the Player Get Mad At?

When a player is told what he has to do to become a better player, does he get mad at the coach, or at himself? If he gets mad at the coach, he'll never get better as a player. If he gets mad at himself, he will get better. It will take some time, but you watch. We had some players at Princeton—I don't want to mention names. I would attack their effort and play. They would get so mad at themselves, and I would tell my assistant coaches, that guy is not going to be a problem; it's just a matter of time. And he would come through. It happened that way every time. What you stress and what the human element is determine the results you get. That is the key to success.

Michael Jordan (seems I mention his name a lot!) plays hard every day; he guards his man, he rebounds, passes, shoots, dribbles—he is unbelievable. Obviously, there are a lot of athletes coming into the NBA who are not like that, and who, as far as talent is concerned, can never be like that. But they can become more like that—or can they? Can they change? Now you go back to the human element, and to the big point in coaching: How is the human being inside this player going to behave? (Remember how I define "behave": to act wisely.)

Motivating Players

People ask me for my psychology on motivating athletes. I don't believe in all that motivational stuff. I cause the tension on my teams. If I had to stop and think about everything I said before I said it to them, I would have been a psychologist. I don't try to psyche them. I just tell them what is on my mind very emphatically. I tell them their good points and I tell them their bad points.

My friend Marvin Bressler, an emeritus professor of sociology at Princeton and a great fan of basketball over the years, likes to remind me of the time I got on one of Princeton's best players ever, Armond Hill, who was drafted in the first round and had a nice career with the Atlanta Hawks. I really admired

Armond both as a player and a person, but I chewed him out at halftime once. I was talking about it with Marvin after the game, feeling a little bad because I thought maybe I had been too harsh and too personal, in front of the whole team. Marvin listened, took a puff on the pipe he always carries, and suggested that since I had berated Hill in front of the other players, I should apologize to him in their presence as well. At the next team practice, I gave an extended apology to the effect that Armond was the best point guard in the Ivy League, and even Larry Bird sometimes threw a bad pass, and that since nobody was perfect, I regretted my remarks of the previous weekend. Well, I had finished my apology, and then it occurred to me to add that when I had yelled at him at Maryland for passing up easy shots, he did deserve that. And when I had lit into him at Michigan he deserved that, too. Marvin told me later that he thought maybe my reverting to my usual role had a comforting effect on my players, as if to reassure them that I hadn't suddenly lost my head.

I think that there are two things about my forcefulness: My criticism is accurate and it's always honest. I don't praise them for doing what they know they can and should do in the first place. I always had trouble with my teams, and when we differ we usually differ over our definitions of fun. You have to be good at what you do, or else how can you have fun? I start each season not knowing how much they can give, but I know it is more than they think. Work is the main factor in their success. That is where their character comes out.

I tell the players they have to share. You have to worry less about yourself and more about the team. In a team sport like basketball, every time you help somebody else, you help yourself. What an incredible irony. You can have no hang-up

70

about points. You can only play if the letter "I" is nonexistent in your vocabularies. Each has to understand what contribution each can make, when to shoot, when not to shoot. As a player, your courses of action are more limited because you belong to a team. When you do something that helps someone else to do something, then when it comes to doing something for yourself, it is easier to do.

If you're on offense and you have the ball in hand and only one idea in mind—to do a certain thing yourself like shoot or drive—you alert the defense to what it is you're trying to do, and that makes it harder for you because they're going to try to stop you. But when you have the ball and you're ready to do other things, like pass to another player, then the defense has to try to stop all those possible things and not just you and your thing. It's amazing how this idea comes out in a game.

The toughest kind of player to motivate is the guy who thinks he is the sun and his teammates are the planets and they revolve around him. The easiest guy is the one who understands he is part of the world and wants to do what's right for the benefit of everyone.

What It Takes to Be Extraordinary

There are certain students who are great in the library. They are in there all the time. Growing up in Bethlehem, I saw the best pool shooters, and what I noticed is they were always playing pool. It's hard for me to believe anyone can be good at anything unless he really goes for it—even at a place like Princeton, which has great students. Very few of them are scholars—people who love learning for the sake of learning and are always in the library. They are the ones, for the most part, who will become better at scholarship.

Geoff Petrie was a great example of this concept applied to basketball. He and I had a little bit of a rough time in the beginning. He had a tendency to be emotional if he didn't play well. That bothers anybody who wants to be as good as he wanted to be. Our problems revolved around my trying to show him a more simple and functional way to do everything he was doing. Basically, I had a different vision for him from the one he had for himself. If I hadn't tried to change him, it would have been a lot easier, but I tried to make him a different person. I saw greatness there, and I wanted to help him find better ways of doing things, to develop more precision in his game. I wanted him to look to the other guy, not to think so much of himself, put a little brainpower into his game. I helped him make the transition from forward to guard, taught him a couple of dribble moves, and to see the game through my eyes. He could do everything including go for the jugular, kill the other guy, beat his brains out, try to beat him so badly he would want to give up the game. He could have had a greater career at Princeton if I had been a better coach at the time, and if he had not gotten hurt. He had a great junior year, but he hurt his back, then hurt his ankle and missed some games. We were going out to play in a tournament at UCLA and it looked like he was out, but I asked him to come along anyway because I knew the guys would want to see him with them. We were shooting around before our first game that night with Indiana and he tells me his back feels pretty good. He plays and scores 31 points. The next night we lose to UCLA and he has 38. Against Columbia his junior year, when we needed to win both games to win the Ivy title, he scored 30 points in each game. He was a fabulous player.

Satisfaction

What gives me the most satisfaction as a coach is bringing together people who have divergent backgrounds and getting them to achieve a goal by sacrificing and integrating their skills. And, of course, I like to win. It brings everybody together.

Sometimes You Can, Sometimes You Can't

I am often asked, How do you get a player to do what he doesn't want to do? Well, sometimes you can, and sometimes you can't. Sometimes reason will work and he will work on his shortcomings. Generally speaking, if he wants to be good, he will try to do the things that you tell him will have a positive effect on what happens to him. For example, you might tell him to hold the ball differently from where he starts his shot. What I notice sometimes—with young kids in particular—is that the players want immediate success. Maybe circumstances are such that they get it, but then, as soon as they don't, they abandon the change and go back to doing it the same way they did before. If a person is intelligent enough to understand that when he is shooting the ball too many of his shots are not going in and you have exhausted all the different reasons as to why that might be the case, and now it comes down to the fact that he may have to reconstruct his shot: Hold the ball in a different spot, maybe lower, higher, maybe his elbow sticks out, or there's not enough rotation, or he's not getting his legs into his shot—in other words, if he's intelligent enough to understand that nothing is working and a change has to be made in his shot, he will go along with it and try to improve.

Other players are very stubborn and will not change because the way they do it is good enough as far as they are concerned. It might be defense, conditioning, overplaying somebody—whatever it is, you try to point out the advantages of making the change.

One of the axioms that go with this is that, generally, the more basic the change, the harder it is to do and therefore the harder it is to convince the player to do it. People prefer to do things that are easier rather than harder.

If the player doesn't want to change and you have exhausted all reason, then, in a competitive situation, you have someone take his place and he doesn't play. If he wants to play, maybe his friends will help him understand the need to change.

I remember in high school, I had a player who shot the ball every time he got it. He never noticed it and nothing I did could convince him to change his habits. So I had a meeting of everybody except him. I told the players that for the next couple of days I didn't want them to throw the ball to him. So they didn't. The guy went crazy for two days: yelling, clapping, complaining, moaning. Finally, he came to see me and I told him the obvious: You never throw to them; now you know what it feels like. That changed things. You can bet that most of the time, if I ask a guy to change, there is a good reason for it. Usually a guy who doesn't want to go along with what I ask quits the team. He might not have as much talent, or he wants to do other things, like play Nintendo or skateboard.

Play to Win

There's a difference between the guys who play to win and those who play not to lose. A big difference. When you play to win, you do all of the extra things that maybe aren't visible, but the result is that you come out on top. When a team plays to win, the shooter who shoots better is going to take more shots—and conversely, the player who doesn't make that many shots won't shoot as much; he understands his role and how he relates to the other players, and so he, too, is playing to win by subordinating his needs to those of the team.

Character

I believe that the essence of character is what I call mental and physical courage. By mental courage I mean, say you are a skilled shooter but have missed five shots, you are down by two points, you are wide open—will you take the sixth, or pass it off? Give me the kid who will take that sixth shot—that is mental courage. We were playing Yale and Sean Jackson went 0 for 8. The next night we played Brown and Sean missed his first five shots, so now he was 0 for 13. I called for him to shoot off a pick and he drilled it. He was tough enough to shoot that ball.

Physical courage is where you are so exhausted you cannot move, yet you keep moving. Or you get elbowed in the face going in for a rebound and you go back in there again. The highest level of the game requires those traits.

Core Toughness

Every team needs a certain amount of toughness. You have to know how to behave when you're behind and how to behave when you're ahead. It's a characteristic I always tried to instill in my teams. In high school and college, each kid must be part of that core of toughness, or it breaks down.

I have always admired physical courage, players who'll dive on the floor for a loose ball, rebounders who can't jump a lick but go after the ball with the attitude that they're going to get it regardless. I remember an incident once in a high school practice game, when I was coaching Gary Walters.

Gary jumped to shoot the ball, had his legs knocked out from under him, and fell on his head, suffering a concussion, although we didn't know that at the time. He saw stars and became nauseated. He was afraid to tell me and continued to play. A few minutes later, he felt faint. He decided he had better tell me something. It was a Saturday morning practice and I told him to lift weights and go home. He lifted weights and then left the gym. It was snowing, and his legs felt so weak he had to get down on his knees and crawl home. When he arrived at his front door, he stood up so his folks wouldn't know, walked in the house, and passed out.

In his senior year, Joey Scott ('87), who was my assistant coach at Princeton and played guard for me, went to the trainer with a bad knee—the ligament was practically all gone in his knee—and the doc told him he was done for the year. Next thing, I see him on the floor with his whole leg bandaged. He scored 16, 18 points. The next night, same thing all over, and he scores 16 points and we win. That's physical courage.

Growing Up with Courage

One of the bad aspects of competition is that it is not always fair. An opponent may bully you, trying to intimidate you, but you have to demonstrate physical courage and hang in there, maybe get an elbow in the face, or take an offensive charge, or get whacked on a rebound. Everybody has the potential for courage, but some people—because they have had to demonstrate it all their lives—are good at it, whereas others are not until the need suddenly arises and they have to learn how to react. A player doesn't like to hear that he's afraid. When I have to tell a player that, I preface it by saying that everyone's afraid of something. You have to decide whether you want to make a commitment to change, to stop being afraid. Education is changing behavior.

I once had a player who was afraid of everything. He shied away from contact in games, and his teammates started kidding him about it. I brought it up to him. When his problem was exposed, he couldn't stand himself. He got mad at himself. By the time he was through, he wasn't afraid of anything. He had the willingness to change, the desire to make himself better. Basketball brings out the need for courage, the need for the kind of response that kids from a lower socioeconomic background are used to every day. That's why the game is dominated by them.

South Bethlehem

The city of Bethlehem in Pennsylvania is the main influence on my life. I was born and raised there, went to high school there, and coached my first college game at Lehigh. It was a big basketball, football, and soccer town, with lots of Portuguese, Mexican, and Spanish families drawn by jobs in the steel mills. It was a great life growing up on the south side. Smoke from the furnaces, the noises from the drop forge and the blast furnaces were ever present when you went to sleep at night. If you ran your finger along the window, you left a trail in the coal dust that came from the smokestacks. And you know what I remember the most? All the church bells ringing at the same time. That was a great sound, even though they were not in tune musically. They rang at five o'clock and you knew it was time to go home for dinner.

My father's job in the steel mills as a first helper in the open-hearth called for shoveling dolomitic materials into wheelbarrows, 500 pounds at a time, or catching red-hot ingots with tongs. He was always coming home with burns on him, and my sister and I would rub butter or lard on his skin. He drank hard whiskey, a lot of it, but he never missed a day of work for sickness and I have never missed a practice or game because of illness, either. He deserves credit for insisting that his children not wind up the way he did.

It was very important to him that we be smart. My sister graduated twelfth in her high school class of 700. I wasn't the student she was, but I could get good grades when I needed to.

We grew up in the Spanish community where there was an open door for my sister and me; wherever we went, there was always food for us. Somebody always seemed to be looking out for us. I try to transfer that sense of community to my team. I want my players to look out for each other, to have pluck, discipline, and love for one another. They do fend for each other. They have a natural feeling of being together, playing together. And when they do, I feel like I've given them a little piece of South Bethlehem, Pa.

What Is Genuine and What Is Not

Nobody ever says anything about team camaraderie when it is genuine because then it's assumed. Like Lombardi once said about winning: Beware of the coach who always talks about winning. Winning, team camaraderie—they are part of an attitude, a consequence of believing and doing the right things. It's like when a player says he gives 110 percent, you can bet he gives 30. Or when a player, a pro, says one minute that he really loves his coach, and then two weeks later signs a bonus with another team. Or when a coach gets fired and his players tell him they loved him. If they loved him, why didn't they play harder? It's perverse, but when you hear talk about caring and stuff like that, to me those are some of the best ways to know there is not enough caring. But when there is, when there are teamwork and understanding, you see the results on the floor; it doesn't need to be praised, or mentioned in words. It's there for the eyes to see.

Greed

Everybody makes such a big deal today about team play because there's such a scarcity of it. Greed is a reason. You have to understand the influence of greed. The great economic teachers of our time have never given consideration to greed. I once got a low grade in economics because I said there was not enough sociology in economics; by that I meant that economics does not account for how hard a guy works, or does not work, or what he does to help his co-workers. A player has to be selfish in the pursuit of the development of his skills, but he cannot be selfish when it comes time to blend them in with what is good for his team.

Team Concept Redefined

It has become a cliché of the modern game to talk about "team concept" but does today's player understand what that really means? In the past each player could do a little bit more individually than he can today and still be a team player. In those days the players didn't talk about team concept; they just did it. Today, more players seem to talk about it than do it. I've mentioned Patrick Ewing, who I think is the consummate team player. Somebody drives down the hole, Ewing steps in front to take the charge. There is a team player, but I don't hear him talking about it. He just does it. And that's the way it was in the past.

■　■　■

Necessity Is the Mother of Invention

As a kid in Bethlehem, I lived right near the railroad tracks. I never got tired because I was always outside playing. Our playground was a coal yard. We invented so many games out of nothing. We played basketball in the beginning with a hoop nailed to a garage door, using a tennis ball. The coal bins had high brick walls, and we played kick ball and chase in them, or goose ball with a tennis ball—games that we invented on the spot. We tightroped along the walls playing tag, and jumped into the piles of coal that were dumped there by train cars. We played Nimbly on the railroad tracks, laying a sharpened segment of a broom handle on a rail, hitting the point to make it fly up, then swatting it for a double or triple or home run. We raced along the rails to see how far we could run without falling and without touching the ties. We swam in both the Lehigh Canal and the river, and at night, we sneaked into the mills and climbed the mountains of minerals and slid down them. We chased rats behind the apartments.

Being poor in South Bethlehem enhanced our ability to develop our creativity. Being poor today engenders violence. One of the basic differences today is that the support groups are shot; no one, except people who live with the terror of it, knows the role of drugs and their effect on kids and families and communities. It's devastating.

Life seemed a lot simpler when I was a kid. I wore the same pair of pants for three years, and when I got holes in my shoes I used to stuff cereal box tops into them. Even when you got hurt, things seemed simpler. I was on a picnic once in Saucon Park in Bethlehem with my father and mother, and was playing in a tree when I fell and hurt my leg. My mother wanted to take me to a doctor. "Don't make a baby out of him," my father said, pulling my leg to show her it was okay. The next day it hurt more, but a friend of my father's had a cure: Soak a piece of meat in egg and wrap it around the leg. My father got a steak and wrapped it around the leg. Another day went by and the pain became worse, and the steak turned putrid. After three days, my father took off the meat bandage. My leg had turned blue. He told me to walk but I couldn't. My mother finally called the doctor, who found that my leg was broken. (I said things seemed simpler, not necessarily wiser.)

As I grew older, we hopped the freights and rode them around South Mountain to Saucon to play basketball and swim. I joined the Boys Club, where I played basketball. Sometimes when we forgot our membership cards, we'd sneak into the club through a bathroom window. I went to the club right after school every day until I left for college. I went home to eat dinner and returned to the club in the evening until the club closed at nine. It was never too hot in the summer to play even though the gym was like an oven. I remember that Chuck Bednarik, the great football player who played both ways for the University of Pennsylvania and the Philadelphia Eagles, belonged to the same club. I was playing against him in a game one summer and he knocked me through one of the open windows of the gym onto a roof below. My best friend Rocco Calvo, who later played quarterback at Cornell, and I would work out on the fields at Saucon. He'd throw me a pass. As soon as I caught the ball, I'd place it at my feet and sprint upfield while Calvo raced to get to the ball and throw me another pass. We'd play basketball, one-on-one, for milkshakes. We just played and played and played.

I was always a hard worker and I viewed playing sports as a privilege, not a right. When you come from a poor family like

I did, and like a lot of kids do today, one outlet for all your energies and emotions seems to be athletics. When you're poor, athletics becomes crucial. It helps you get out of the slums, go to college, get a degree. Basketball allowed me to go to college. I had already learned the value of good grades —if I got a C on my report card, my coach wouldn't let me play basketball in high school. My father taught me that it's very important to do what you're supposed to do and not reduce your standards just because it's something you don't especially like doing.

I had three terrific coaches: in junior high school, high school, and college, and they all had an impact, to the extent that it would have been enough for me and what I wanted to do with my life to have been like any of them. I don't know if coaches today have the same impact on their players. My high school coach was Joseph Preletz and he was truly amazing. He had no real background to speak of, but he was forty years ahead of his time. He was totally organized and the things he had us doing were unbelievable. This was the '40s and he had us all-court pressing, playing a 1-3-1 zone and using a delay game. We went 24-3 in both my junior and senior years and I made all-state. Coach Preletz had such an impact on me that after I graduated from college, my ambition was to become a teacher and go back to my school and coach the basketball team. If I could ever had been hired as the head coach at my high school, I might not have ever left Bethlehem.

■　■　■

The Socioeconomics of Basketball

In Bethlehem, athletics used to be dominated by the poor kids from the South Side, the sons of the early immigrants. The great preponderance of players today come from the lower socioeconomic level of our society. Once, the game of basketball was dominated by poor Jewish kids from sections of New York City. Today, it is African-American players. It's not a racial thing; it has to do with economic forces. Basketball is played well by people who are poor—who come from the poor sections of town, from the streets.

You ask what do they value most in terms of their daily lives: manliness, courage, cunning, stealth, trickery, whatever it is that they have to have to survive. The middle class takes pride in citizenship and doing well in school. The upper classes live on the other side of town and have their three meals, drive to school in a car, go to the dentist regularly, and worry about following the family line—all those things that any upper socioeconomic class has, but the lower classes never have. So when a baseball is being thrown at you at 100 miles per hour, what does it take? It takes what the lower-class people, the South Side people, took pride in. Or, when you go in for a rebound and somebody smashes you in the nose, or somebody threatens you, what does it take? Not civic pride. A lower-class guy has been threatened from childhood. He fights back. He fights to survive. And all those traits come in handy when you play basketball, or baseball, or football. They show up.

That doesn't mean there aren't exceptions. John McPhee, the writer who's a basketball fan and a friend of mine, said it best in his book about Bill Bradley when he was a player at

Princeton: He said Bradley had to overcome the fact that his father was president of a bank—had to overcome "the handicap of wealth"—to become the great player he was.

Take every black pro basketball player who has moved into an affluent suburb, into the three-car-garage-plus-swimming-pool neighborhood, and find out how many of their sons are going to be great athletes like their fathers. Black or white, it makes no difference: Their sons don't often make it to the pro level. Once the father reaches a certain income, those things he might once have done on an everyday basis become alien to his kin. Scholastic achievement takes precedence over athletic prowess. No, it's not racial so much as economic. Once the economic status of Jewish parents in New York began to improve, that culture's dominance of the game declined. There are some international players from overseas who do well here because they come from the same type of background without the advantages that so many American players have growing up.

When I Played

As a player, I loved to shoot, to drive—I loved to play. I played as well as I could. I never second-guessed my effort. Even when I had the grippe and was told by doctors to stay in bed for four days, I went out to practice. I was so weak the coach asked me if I had stayed up late drinking.

I like the idea of the ball going through the hoop. I like the idea of running, stealing balls, dribbling, passing, and I like the competition. To me, basketball is a terrific game and I just loved playing it. I played baseball and football, but I stood around a lot in baseball, and in football I got knocked around and was a little scared.

Basketball seemed to have something pretty about it: You're looking at a guy, or a combo of guys who can dribble, pass, and shoot, and you see the ball fly through the air and someone catches it, and they work together using all their skills, their legs, arms, hands, heads—all the parts of the human body, the teamwork, the understanding that goes into playing together as a team—that's what makes it different from some other sports. It is very emotional for me. When you're playing with a bunch of guys and there's genuine friendship, that isn't an intellectual experience. It's emotional and it comes from the sense of respect and happiness you feel in the company of your teammates. Knowledge has nothing to do with that. Bring those emotional qualities out onto the floor and add your own skill level to that of the team—there is nothing like that.

I love the soar. I love to see a player like Brian Taylor take off from the foul line and soar like a plane going up—I love to watch guys that have this way of jumping that they seem to keep going up and up as if they'll never come down. That's something special, and I never had enough of that at Princeton. Geoff Petrie was one of the best at getting up and never coming down.

And there's the joy of watching a beautiful passer who has a sense of where to throw the ball, or watching a guy play who knows what he's going to do with the ball before he catches it —those players are fun to watch. I like to see the movement of the ball. The Chicago Bulls are a great example—a lot of their stuff is one-on-one but starts with basic movement of the ball. Eventually, by moving the ball around, someone gets a good shot.

After forty-three years of coaching, I still love the movement of the ball and all that it entails for the game, and if I were alive to coach another forty years, assuming the game was still in existence, those feelings and the principles they embody would remain the same. When there's movement of the ball, then there's movement of the defense and things start happening: You get some wide-open shots, some drives, some back doors and front, or on-side ball cuts—you get so much movement, and it's hard to guard someone moving. The epitome of great basketball is five guys passing, cutting, moving the ball, doing what's natural and not fighting for possession of the ball.

Lafayette

I went to college to play basketball. The great thing about Lafayette was that the faculty had other ideas. I had great teachers there. I had an English professor named Donald McCluskey who inspired you to learn. I had a history professor named Arthur Minnich who made you feel that you were letting him down if you didn't learn. The best guidance of all came from Sam Pascal, a language professor. He loved athletics. He was an inspiration to a lot of kids at Lafayette. I was just a fair player at Lafayette until the second big influence in my basketball career came along—Coach Van Breda Kolff. He was something special. He was not yet the great coach he was going to be, but he was very wise. He taught me how to be organized, how to evaluate things, how to know what was important and what was not, and most of all, how to see the game differently from the way I had.

On Being 5′ 6¾″ Tall

Why is it that every interviewer asks me whether I ever played basketball? It's funny. Sometimes they can't visualize me as a basketball player because of my size.

The only times that you as a coach ever want to make size an issue with a small player would be for his own protection. You would be trying to help him survive and do well with the size problem. It's difficult. I'm 5′ 6¾″ tall, so I was a small player at Lafayette. The size differential is even more telling now. The guards are so big, 6′ 5″, 6′ 6″, and it's so much harder to be a small player and succeed at the highest level. You can do it in college, but as the level of competition increases so does the difficulty for the small player. The challenges become more severe. You do have guys who are small who excel—most of the time, they are extremely fast and have some kind of specialty that makes them succeed and overcome their lack of size.

One thing that I know is true for all small guys, and it helps them an awful lot, is that they never think they're small. At no time did I ever hear a small guy complain about being small. I never did. There are some sports where if you weigh 118 pounds you can still be successful—you can wrestle at 118 with someone of the same weight, or play shortstop if you're 5′ 7″. In those and other cases, the number of times that your height becomes a factor isn't anywhere as numerous as in basketball.

When you're short, the first thing an opposing team does is make you guard someone 6′ 6″ underneath the basket, and that's hard to do, really hard to do. In college you can play zone so a small player never goes underneath the basket, but you can't play zone in the pros. You must be fast and versatile as hell. And you must be able to score. You cannot be intimidated when you're small. You have to go out to play and do well and that's it. A guy who is 6′ 10″ or 7′ 1″ and slow is in trouble but he still thinks he should be playing. A guy who is 5′ 6″ and slow doesn't even think about playing.

Coaching Taller Players

People ask me from time to time if I feel awkward coaching centers and forwards who are often a foot taller than I. I have several little rules in life. One is that I never go anywhere I do not belong. If I go into the pivot, you can bet I know where I am going, and when I get there, you can bet I am going to know what I'm talking about.

Coaching at Reading

My first year at Reading High School was the first year that I felt wrapped up with a school and a town that loved basketball beyond what you could understand. Every game was a sellout, and it was rare in the playoffs to have a crowd of less than 9,000. I coached and taught there for eight years. It was an important learning experience and I made friends there I'll never forget. If coaching and teaching weren't so hard, I might still be there, but when you have five classes to teach and have to practice at night—eight years there was like twenty in college.

My practices started at 5:30 P.M. with the jayvees and lasted until 9:00 P.M., with the varsity coming in at seven. I held Saturday practices, and at first I made them voluntary, but no one came, so I made them mandatory. I was very strict. I had a player who got caught playing cards in school once. I told him if it happened again, I would drop him from the team. He got caught again so I kicked him off. His father went to see the principal but the principal backed me. I also didn't like fancy stuff on the court, like behind-the-back passes, which were anathema to me. I had forgotten this, but Gary Walters reminded me recently that he dribbled behind his back one time during his high school career. It happened to be in a game that was attended by Coach Van Breda Kolff, who was scouting him for Princeton. I thought Walters was showing off and removed him from the game.

I've calmed down a lot since the days when I was at Reading, but I still get upset when I see poor execution, or see players not trying hard, or giving only half an effort. I'll get upset over those things if I live to be 100, but I'm not as rough as I was at Reading.

■ ■ ■

Why Practice?

In every little drill, if you care enough to put maximum effort into it, almost everyone improves. The key is to make sure all drills are relevant. Certain guys don't go full speed in practice—some NBA stars hate to practice. But you don't hear that about Michael Jordan, and didn't about Larry Bird when he played. There has to be something useful about practice, otherwise why do it? I told my players I wanted 2½ hours of basketball from them every day. It's not like some places where the players sleep late, mess around until practice, and are fresh and ready for three hours of practice. My guys had to give me 2½ hours after a long day of classes. We didn't have meetings. They're like committees.

We always spent a half hour on the fundamentals of dribbling, passing, and shooting. We then broke down into offense and defense and the sets we planned to use for the coming game. Repetition is the key to success—doing what you have to do over and over and always doing it right.

I run a rough practice because the more you do in practice, the less you have to do in a game. And it gives players on your team who normally are not going to play in a game a chance to improve. Another reason is that a hard practice creates a little tension, so that when it comes time to play in a game, they're already used to some tension.

Defense Is the Heart of the Game

When I talk about basketball technique and strategy, about my way of playing the game, I begin with defense because defense is the heart of our game. Good defense is recognizable even when you're losing.

The object of my defensive strategy is to contest every pass and shot, to force the opponent to move the ball under continuous pressure. I want the other team to play offense longer than they're used to. If you react to ball movement a microsecond faster than usual and keep your hands up, they have to try another pass, then still another. That makes them anxious. They commit fouls and they make mistakes. Most teams can't pass well, or be patient for very long, so they'll eventually rush a shot, and then we've won the battle.

Defense is not a variable. It's a constant. Defense has to be deeply embedded in your attitude. It is something you can do well every time—both the individual and the team. A good defensive player plays good defense almost all the time. Shooting is a variable; 50 percent of the time you miss. Contesting a jump shot is not a variable. Skill is a variable. Work is not a variable, not a skill; it's an attitude. In my career, because my players have seldom been blazing fast, they have had to compensate with hard work.

It helps to be quick, and to have long arms. A guy who has long arms gets to the ball faster, and gets in the way of more passes. You can recover from your mistakes when you're quick. All things being equal, you always want to pick the faster guy—if he has the desire.

There is a technical part and a life part to defensive play. The life part consists of three things that must be very prominent in good defense: courage, intelligence, and energy. If you have a good dose of heart, head, and legs working for you, you can become a good defensive player. If your legs tire out, your heart surrenders and you won't move your legs. When you're tired, do you have the courage to fight through screens?

If you don't use your head, you're in trouble: Defense starts by asking yourself how you guard the man with the ball. What are your attributes as an athlete? Do you move your legs? What do you look at? Do you look at the ball once he dribbles? Can he shoot? Does he go right, left? Does he have an outside shot? Do you expend energy trying to stop a guy from shooting who can't shoot? Even if you're a little slow, you can be a good defensive player as long as you have these attributes to compensate. A guy like Larry Bird, who was a little slow, had these attributes and played excellent team defense.

I used to rely exclusively on man-to-man defense because I thought playing zone was an admission of weakness, that I was saying I couldn't play man-to-man, which requires speed and character. I started getting players who, one, weren't able to keep their bodies in front of the shooters; two, weren't able to contest shots; and three, had a knack for running into screens. It's hard to play man-to-man under those circumstances. In 1979–80, we were on a plane flying back from a tournament in Hawaii, with a record of 2-11. Tony Relvas, my assistant coach, and I were drinking Bloody Marys to forget our woes. The coach of Illinois, who won the tournament and beat the national champ, Louisville, is on the same plane and he comes over to me and says, "Something is wrong with my team." I look at him and call the stewardess over. I said, "Ma'am, does that door to the outside open because I want to jump." We're 2-11 and he's 17-0 and telling me something's wrong with his team. So I just whipped down another Bloody Mary. I said to Tony, "There are three conditions that make a good man-for-man defense. One is you have to contest or pressure the ball. That's key above all else. Two, your guys cannot get picked off and must go over screens. And three, all shots must be contested. Well, our team runs into screens, doesn't contest shots, and doesn't pressure the ball. We gotta play zone."

I had run a 1-2-2 zone in high school so it wasn't too hard to put it in. The manner in which our opponents attacked a zone then was all stereotyped. There wasn't much picking against a zone so that eliminated that problem for us. The zone also minimized the problem of pressuring the ball individually.

The zone we put in caused so much trouble that we went on to win 13 of the next 17, finishing 11-4 in the league, almost winning the title on a shot we missed at the buzzer. We stayed with the zone for about five years. We had a kid, Steve Mills ('81), who could play the point and was good at deflecting passes. After five years, the other teams started to catch on and we had to adjust, and after a decade of making changes we were back to playing man-to-man, which is where we were last season. (My assistants were after me to switch to zone again and I have a feeling Princeton will go to a zone in the future.)

When I went to the zone, it's true that I became less of a purist and played zone to compensate for not having team speed, but it also protected my players in foul trouble and minimized our taking practice time to cover out-of-bounds plays against the many different schemes our opponents used.

I've heard some coaches say they have to "sell" their team on defense before they can teach it. I resent that word "sell" and I've never used it in my life in basketball. You must SHOW a guy how important defense is. You educate him.

The first principle of teaching defense is to recognize what your players can do defensively. Not all are equally good in all phases of defense, and a coach has to see what the differences are. Some are good at fighting through picks—"going over the top" (which I'll describe in a minute). Others are good at denial defense; others, at counterattack, or waiting until the opponent acts, then reacting. Reggie Bird ('72) was probably one of the best defenders we ever had. For putting pressure on the dribbler, we never had anyone better. But against a team that liked to set picks, he'd get picked off every single time. Joe Heiser ('68), another good defender, had a harder time keeping his body in front of the man he was guarding, but he could slip through every pick.

The second principle is: There is no single absolute. The result counts no matter how you do it. You are not going to be right 100 percent of the time. If you know that, you won't force situations, or force some principle of play that won't provide the same yield as something else. Any defense is good regardless of what it is if it's effective. If the principle is good, it will hold true 85 percent of the time.

I once argued with a coach who was renowned for his zone press. No matter what happened, he never changed his zone press and he got into trouble. I asked him if he had ever heard of General Braddock and his march in the wilderness against the French and Indians. The European style of war was unsuited to America and Braddock got whipped. Not everybody can get over the top of a pick to contest the movement of the ball. No matter how hard a player works, he doesn't seem able to get over the top, so why keep telling him to do it, because then you cause a lot of trouble for the rest of the team? There may be a better way. The pick may be well made, or your guy may be slow. It is not an admission of failure that on occasion you won't and can't fight the pick. For that player, something else is okay.

Fronting the man in the pivot—there's another example of where you may have to violate one of your principles. One of the statistics that is fairly true about basketball is that when you let a guy near the basket get the ball, two things often happen: He either scores, or he gets fouled. So you work hard not to let him get the ball low. You front him, but there are some guys you cannot front, or you cannot front 100 percent of the time. You try to know when to front and when fronting jeopardizes the rest of the defense.

The third principle is for the coach to recognize that the faster a team is, the more pressure it can apply defensively. Speed narrows the court, makes it less long. The court is larger to a slower team. You have to recognize if your team is slow, in which case it's not wise to extend pressure or to try to force turnovers. On the other hand, if you are fast, it would be foolish not to be aggressive and guard your man tightly. The faster guy most often wins the contest for the ball.

The fourth principle is that whatever you emphasize, and to the degree that you do, you get better at it up to the level of your talent. Let's say you develop a defense that prevents easy, unrestricted movement of the ball. You will be better at that than somebody else who doesn't emphasize it—up to the level of your ability.

The fifth principle is that the force of the coach determines the quality and intensity of the defense. I have seen good coaches not get the same level of intensity from the defense that they do from the offense. The personality and dynamism of a Bobby Knight at Indiana are important in getting defense taught. Principles alone do not get the job done. Others might know more defense but don't have the same strength of personality. Knowledge alone is not enough.

Not many coaches understand or appreciate these principles of defense. Their willingness even to listen to them is low. I feel sorry for them, young coaches especially, because they have the propensity to spend too much time tinkering with the offense. What's missing on defense is some clear thinking. I knew I was rarely going to get good physical specimens at Princeton, so I stressed attitude and thinking; that's what we had to work with. Bobby Knight's defense is the most oppressive man defense I have seen or coached against in the past decade. But you can follow Knight around the country for a year lapping up everything he says about defense, and when you play or coach, there is no guarantee you'll be any good. He is only giving you 25 percent of what counts. The rest is attitude. The strength of my Princeton teams has always been attitude, intelligence, and discipline.

Zone Versus Man-to-Man

In a man-to-man, everybody knows what to do: *Guard your man.* In a zone, it's harder to tell who should do what. You start hearing, "Coach, I'm sorry, I thought . . ." When you start getting that, you're dead.

Defensive Fundamentals

I've never thought that much about the defensive stance. I would emphasize it more with younger kids—try to get a seventh-grade kid in a good athletic stance, a boxer's stance, with the legs the same distance as shoulder width, ready to move in all directions. Get low, but don't get so low you cannot move; don't stand up so straight that your man will drive by you. You want to keep your man in front of you if he has the ball; if he doesn't, you want to stand in such a way that you can deny him the pass if you want to.

When the man you're guarding has the ball, what do you look at—the eyes or the ball? I tell my guys to look at the guy and see everything until he starts to dribble. Once he starts to dribble, look at the ball, because to do anything with the ball, like shoot, or pass, or dribble, he has to pick it up.

I've seen players who have a great stance and do not defend. They reach down and slap the floor, tuck their pants, and get ready to guard while their opponent blows right by them. What you have to do on defense is you must be ready to defend, which means you must be disposed to guard your man. When you're ready to guard someone, you're ready to contest or combat whatever you see him trying to do. I think the basic thing on defense is to defend the obvious, meaning what you know he is going to do.

I was asked once to speak at a clinic about defense—these were young kids. I asked for a volunteer to come down and let me set him up in a defensive stance. He assumed his stance and then I asked the other kids to help me critique it. We spent fifteen minutes adjusting this and that, and then when everyone felt his stance was just perfect, I sent the kid back to the stands and told them: None of that has anything to do with playing defense. Defense is head, heart, and legs.

If you want to learn how to guard your opponent up to the level of your ability, you have to start by guarding somebody who has the ball. That brings the processes of the head, heart, and legs into play, as opposed to drilling over and over on how to have the right stance, or how to slide around the court, with no concept of what you are doing as a defender and what he is going to do as an offensive player.

I tell my players to use their stance and play one-on-one. That's a great drill: You have to keep your body in front of your man, contest what he does, know something about him, force him left, right, make him shoot—the cerebral side of the game comes into play—you're now defending what you know he can do. I never spent too much time in sliding around the court in an imaginary defensive stance following the directions of a coach or leader in front of a group. My philosophy and feelings on sliding drills are a little controversial: Basically I feel that if you want to learn how to guard your man, you learn that by guarding a man.

You can play one-on-one, two-on-two, and work on sliding, going over the top, and switching. Then you can move to three-on-three, add post drill defense, etc. It could be that an individual player on his own during the off season might want to do a sliding drill to strengthen his legs or improve his lateral movement, yet even here I think by guarding someone he'd pick up all those things in a more realistic and pragmatic situation.

Keeping your hands up on defense is one thing, but doing something with them is another. I've seen players who look great with their hands up but aren't using them to defend. You hear coaches instructing their players: "Don't reach and don't foul." I feel that when coaches say not to reach with your hands on defense, they're taking away three feet of defense for each arm. They are doing it because they're afraid you might reach and get off balance and make it easier for the offensive man to go around you and for you to foul him. But hands that are raised and moving close off passing lanes and cause distraction. When you deflect a pass, or contest a dribble, or make the opponent miss a shot, now your hands are doing something. Nothing is more intimidating than deflecting passes. It makes a passer very tentative. I say that if you don't use your hands, you're committing a bigger sin and aren't as effective defensively. My view on this is also controversial.

I like to see a defender fight to get his body between the dribbler who is screening and the man for whom he's screening. That's what I call "going over the top." The object is not to let the dribbler hand off the ball to his man. I like to think that if the defender can get one leg and one arm in between the screen and the ball, he can push through and get between the ball and his man. It is very aggressive defense because you're contesting every pass, every movement of the ball, every shot—we're especially trying to see that good shooters don't get the ball behind the screen where they can shoot a free shot.

Not everyone can go over the top with equal effectiveness. You want to play aggressive defense, but if your team is slow, maybe it can't. Then you have to think about sliding through, which is less aggressive and means you avoid screens, permit handoffs or a pass, then play the player after he catches the ball. This is not necessarily bad when you're guarding someone who can't shoot.

If you want to press as a defensive tactic, you look at your own strengths and the first thing you check is your speed. When you press, you stretch the court from end to end and you want to be sure you're fast enough to cover the entire court. You also look to see if your team has athletes who can anticipate, who can see what the other team is trying to do. These are players who are aggressive by nature, and who can react well. You also want players who love to run and don't get tired. I like to see if they possess the joy that goes with running and contesting the ball the entire game. It helps, too, if you have some long arms to block passing lanes.

100

Then you look at the other team. You might notice they don't have good ball handlers, or maybe they only have one or two, in which case the odds are that eventually they'll throw the ball to someone who doesn't know what to do with it when he catches it. You want to press a team like that. A team with four or five ball handlers is rough as heck to press—they're always throwing the ball to someone who can do something with it.

One goal in pressing might be to make the other team shoot fast, especially if they want to hold the ball to counteract your offense. You want them to shoot fast, so you can control the tempo of play. You also press to try to force turnovers. Go after steals. Get a layup. Excite the crowd. Create fear, confusion, break down their discipline—all that stuff shows up when you press.

Almost always when you have a fast player, you can pressure the ball. Sean Jackson was like a bulldog on the press. He'd go right for the outlet pass. He was unreal. We devised a press around him that was highly unusual—basically, we denied the ball to the opposing point guard. Because the game has become so specialized and you may have only one player who handles the ball, if you don't let him handle the ball you can cause trouble.

Dean Smith has been pressing for years at North Carolina. Nolan Richardson of Arkansas has long been an exponent of the full-court press—he calls his defense "forty minutes of hell" and it's just that. He also has strong guys who are very fast. We've usually been a little too slow to press. We pressed with Brian Taylor, because he was so fast. He stole lots of balls. So did Reggie Bird, who used to make a habit of coming into the game as a sixth man and stealing the ball two or three times right away. But, for the most part, except for an occasional player like Sean Jackson, I didn't have that kind of foot speed at Princeton.

When you deny your man access to the ball—you don't let him catch it—you are playing denial defense. The defender in this case has to see the ball, even though his back is turned to the passer almost exclusively as opposed to being in an open stance where you form a triangle with the three points being you, your opponent, and the ball. An open stance means you point with one hand to the man you are defending, and with the other hand to the man with the ball. Your chest is open to the ball. In a closed stance, your back is to the ball and you are in denial defense.

Truth is, you can take whatever defensive philosophy you want and reverse it and a forceful coach will make it work. You can say, "Force the offense down the side of the court." Works pretty good. Or force it into the middle—that works pretty good, too. It's mostly attitude and effort that make a defense successful. But one thing—putting pressure on the ball—has more of an impact than any philosophical discussion of how to guard a man, or how to go over the top, or defend the back screen. If each player, when he guards his man, can press him, put pressure on him, you'll disturb passes and intimidate your opponents.

Defending the Pivot

Man-you-ball. That is the cryptic version of our defensive philosophy. It means keep the proper distance at an angle between yourself and the man you are guarding, and the man with the ball. Except when you're defending in the pivot—

then you depart from man-you-ball in that you are directly in between the ball and your man. Generally speaking, if you play behind the pivot man, he's going to score and you're going to foul. I like to try to front the man in the pivot, or high-side him, and prevent him from catching the ball. It's rarely done in the pros because the lane is so wide that when you front the guy, he has an easy roll to the basket. Also, the rules are such that you don't get the weak-side help that you do in college. That's why you see so many pro teams playing in back of the pivot, though when the ball is thrown down to the low post, then they double on the ball—someone comes from somewhere, one in front and one in back.

A lot of times, I just look at a guy and see how he does defending the pivot before I decide what to do. For example, I had one guy a few years ago who was a pretty good player but he couldn't front anyone. He would get in front of the pivot and the offense would lob a pass over his head to the pivot man, who sometimes was even shorter than my man. He couldn't seem to jump fast enough to stop that. I have had other guys, like Kit Mueller ('91), who was so strong, no one could push him around, so he could guard much taller guys down low. This is another area where you may believe in a certain principle of defense concerning how you defend the pivot, but the strategy you eventually choose depends on the abilities of your player. Your principles have to be guided by the results.

■ ■ ■

Legs Don't Lie

If you place ten players behind a screen in such a way that I can see their legs, I'll pick out the best players seven out of ten times by the way they move their legs, the constant motion, the quickness of their feet. Good players are always moving their legs.

Stern Discipline

The sterner the discipline, the greater the devotion. You cannot equate athletics with war, but you want to create the kind of camaraderie that develops between two men on the front lines—what they go through, the sternness of their discipline, their test, and the sense they have of each other. I've always believed that when you ask guys to give more than they think they can give, you provide them the opportunity to develop a level of devotion to each other and to their cause that is greater than it would be in less exacting circumstances. That's the way it's worked for me, at least.

Don't Think It's a Drill

I emphasize to my guys that anything we do in practice is not a drill. If they get to thinking it's a drill, they won't notice it's the same thing that goes on in a game. I have to tell them that what we're doing in practice is exactly what happens in a game. One of my most fundamental points is that we will not do one single thing in practice that doesn't show up in a game. Everything we do in practice must show itself somewhere in the game, or else we don't do it.

What Is the Value of a Drill?

Many coaches like to use a conditioning drill called "ball-busters," where the players race back and forth between two points, touching the floor each time they turn, and gradually extending the distance between the two marks. At a camp one summer, I lined up a group of youngsters at the end of practice and asked how many of them could do ball-busters. They groaned and raised their hands. "Well, you will never do that drill here," I told them. "It might teach you how to be good at picking things up off the ground, but it does not relate to basketball."

If a coach spends a lot of time trying to develop his team's agility and reaction by using a whistle to signal his players to turn, or jump, or move their hands or legs, he might improve their reaction to the whistle but that doesn't really help them guard their men. The best way for them to learn that is to guard their men. To get the best results in anything you teach, teach the specific thing you look for, and the more repetition, the better the guy gets at that thing. Repetition is the mother of learning.

■　■　■

Punctuality

I like guys to be punctual and show up for practice on time. Punctuality in itself is good. In industry, when there is a shortage of jobs, everyone shows up on time. When you're punctual, you're telling your teammates what you think of them. They aren't waiting for you before they can start. That's important.

Locker Room Habits

When I first came to Princeton, Chauncey, the guy who cleaned up our locker room, came to me one day and asked if I would tell my guys to put the tape from their ankle wrappings in the waste can instead of on the floor, and put their sneakers up on top of their lockers so he could mop up. My locker room was always clean—that was important to me, and I wanted to make sure my players didn't make the custodian's job harder and that they showed respect for how well he was cleaning up.

It is unbelievable, but I had to tell my guys about that every year. Here is someone the players know works hard to keep the building clean. I asked my guys: Don't you like to come into this building and see how clean it is? And the next day, the floor has orange peels, tape, sneakers—what is this? So I told them, if you're the guy who is throwing this stuff on the floor, how much trouble is it for you to throw it in the waste can? It's a little thing but it's important.

This kind of behavior shows up in a game: A player who thinks, I don't feel like picking up my tape today, that's the same guy who's going to think, I'm not going to work hard today on the court, or I'm not going to follow the guy on his cut this time, or we got enough points to win and I don't need to work hard any longer. Pretty soon, you find that the guys start doing what they want instead of what they're supposed to do. I don't want any argument from anybody about it because I think I'm right about this.

Drinking and Basketball

People today are down on alcohol, but did you ever notice how many cups of caffeine some people drink? Five or six mugs of coffee, or half a dozen sodas. Compare that to five or six beers. Which is worse? What is worse than caffeine? I would rather they drink two glasses of beer than two sodas with all that sugar and caffeine. The answer is that neither six mugs of coffee nor six beers are necessarily good or right. My philosophy is moderation. Be good at something, right? Well, be good at moderation, too. I don't think the Spartan way—total abstention—has been very successful

I do not make a federal case out of drinking. I tell my guys that the main reason they go out should be to enjoy their friends, not to drink. There has to be a little mischief in athletes. I like to see them have a little cunning, a little cockiness, some self-assertiveness, as opposed to traveling a straight line—although I have had many players who traveled a straight line and were great. The main point is: Avoid excesses. And if you do drink a lot, you had better know what the consequences are. How will it affect you, and if it affects your conditioning, how does that affect the team? Are you

disturbing others? Getting drunk, throwing up, getting sick—
those activities miss the point. The object is to be with your
friends. That's the key.

Autographs

I just don't like autographs. The people who want my
autograph don't do anything with it. It is the most ridiculous
thing I have ever seen. I give it when someone asks, but always
under protest. The guy could be using his time to do better
things than ask for autographs. If a little kid wants me to
autograph a basketball, I would rather have him go play with
the ball.

Relationship Between Athletics and Life

There are some things you will do later in life that
basketball can help you prepare for. How hard do you work
and how much do you contribute to what your group is doing?
As a player, can you say you've left no stone unturned to get
the job done? You worked hard as a player and did all those
extra little things to get better. Now you're a doctor, and you
keep on working to get better.

I think there is a relationship between athletics and life.
Sports do not build character. They reveal character. They can
help you realize who you are, what your potential is, and
maybe what it is you have to change about your habits to

realize your full potential. The fans and the sports world make the mistake of acclaiming a player's success without noticing his work habits, which are a reflection of his character.

The Challenge of Coaching at Princeton

When I was interviewed for the coaching job at Princeton in 1967 I was asked how I would feel coaching in front of 3,000 at Dillon Gym—that was the maximum number the old gym could seat and it was a pretty big crowd at Princeton basketball games in those days. I reminded them that at Reading, I had coached my teams at playoff time in front of crowds of 10,000.

When Princeton hired me, I never thought I could not do the job. I never looked at things as challenges, or set goals, or anything like that. I didn't say to myself, well, I'll stay at Princeton for five years and then move to a bigger school. It was an opportunity that I wanted and I was able to get it, and so, that being the case, you go ahead and do what you've always done, which is to do the best you can. I did not feel intimidated. I knew it was going to be tough following Coach Van Breda Kolff, who had done so well, but I never thought I was going to be overwhelmed. I was concerned that maybe the success they'd had at the time was going to have an impact on the admission process. I think if you get too good in athletics at Princeton it becomes an embarrassment, so they tend to tighten the screws. When Princeton went to the Final Four, some people might have gotten worried that because we'd been so successful, somebody might ask what's going on down there. There are certain schools in our league that wouldn't be bothered by such an accusation, but it would bother Princeton.

Just Do It

Self-confidence is all part of growing up, your childhood, your experience with parents, friends, advisors. When you go to do something, just go ahead and do it and don't make a big thing out of it. Don't think that it is too much or too little. Instead think that because you've decided to do something, you'll do it the best you can. That's why in so many areas, I have never been afraid—like, for example, speaking in front of an audience. I never got nervous. I always felt I had something to say, and if I didn't I wouldn't be there.

So you work every day and what happens is you're happy, reasonably happy, not very happy, unhappy, all the degrees you can go through—you enjoy your work, or you don't enjoy your work. All that is part of it. Are you happy doing what you are doing? If the answer is in the affirmative then you stay, and if you aren't or you feel you're not good enough, then you have to look at that, too.

Fundamentally Unsound

At the college level, when you get a player whose skill level is suspect, you have to devise some way of playing to make up for his shortcomings along those lines. When you're fundamentally unsound, you inhibit the way your team can play. Poor fundamentals restrict the things a coach can teach his kids. Sometimes a player doesn't want to work hard; other times he cannot. A common mistake among youngsters is to settle for less than the most effective level. They don't want to be embarrassed so they settle for less.

What I Found at Princeton

There wasn't anything radical I had to change about Princeton's program. I felt that the players were not as loyal to each other, or as interdependent as they might have been, or as I was used to in high school. That comes more from inexperience than anything else. Even at Lehigh, my players had been a lot closer than at Princeton. The Princeton players did not play in the off season; they went back to their dorms after the season and it didn't seem as though you could get them to the gym to play. Then Geoff Petrie came, and guys started playing with him in the off season, and so, after my being here three or four years, I finally got my players playing pickup ball in the off season. When guys play in the spring or preseason—that interaction increases their camaraderie. That camaraderie was the one thing missing when I became coach here.

Developing camaraderie is harder at a place like Princeton, because there are so many distractions. Also, at Princeton, people constantly ask the players why they're playing such a hard sport when they're here to study. At every university, there are always people who do not believe in the value of athletics. At some places, I don't blame them.

My intensity was a new ingredient there. Coach Van Breda Kolff is one of the premier coaches of all time, and I will always regard him as my coach. But his manner, his sense of independence did not go over with the powers that be, and he didn't get the recognition he deserved—instead, it was Bill Bradley who got credit for taking Princeton to the Final Four of the NCAAs. But then in the two years after Bradley left, Coach Van Breda Kolff's Princeton teams did really well, and he went to the Los Angeles Lakers and took them to the seventh game of the NBA Finals. He was successful wherever he went.

His thing, his goal was to take things as they are and build around them. I take things and if they aren't right for me I try to change them. He might see a player and say that guy doesn't have it or doesn't care enough and he'll just build something around him to make him useful. Me, I want to change the guy, make him better. I don't know if that's a better idea because you have a lot of troubles that way, and trying to change the player may not be successful. It's a lot more pragmatic to do it Coach Van Breda Kolff's way. My intensity level and my belief in the way an organization or friends should be were different from his. Of course, he had gone to school at Princeton and seen what kind of kid went there and where they came from, and I hadn't. As a coach, I had my high school days and one college season at Lehigh to fall back on, but in both places teaching the idea of togetherness was an easy thing compared to Princeton.

I did eventually change things, but I have always had more trouble coaching than Coach Van Breda Kolff did. That's a compliment to him.

■ ■ ■

Communing to Win

During the summer of 1968, when Jadwin Gym was being built, I began to worry that it wasn't going to be completed in time for the season. They had been working on it for three years and they seemed to be in the final stages, when, in midsummer, for no apparent reason, activity seemed to slow down. I decided to visit the gym several times a week. I thought that the workers would perform better if someone who cared about the building and about the quality of their work was there watching.

I remember walking around the unfinished hangar-sized structure with a cigar in my mouth, nodding at the workmen. I watched them put on a lot of the final touches—the maple-wood floor for instance. It was unbelievable how big and magnificent that place was. It was to have three basketball courts and seats for 7,500 people. I had never played or coached in anything like it.

On some days, I went there at sunset when the workers were gone. I would sit on a grass bank and smoke and stare at it. If I had to go away from town, I recruited one of my own kids to go down there and be prepared to report to me by telephone on the work progress. John McPhee likes to tell about the time he called my house in the evening and asked for me. When he learned that I wasn't there, that I had gone down to the new gym, he seemed surprised, especially when he discovered that I went there every night. I guess McPhee figured he had a story in the making because he dropped what he was doing, got some cans of beer, and drove to the Jadwin parking lot just as it was starting to get dark. I don't remember this, and you have to remember he gets paid for telling stories, pretty good stories. But he says he found me sitting on a retaining wall by the construction site and that I seemed lost in thought and didn't notice him. He sat down beside me without speaking, and handed me a can of beer, which he says I opened without looking at it, or at him, or saying anything, still staring at the unfinished gym. We sat like this without talking for a while—McPhee says half an hour. I guess at some point after the gym had become a dark shadow, I suddenly broke the silence and asked him, "Could you imagine having a losing season in there?" You know what's funny? I can believe that story.

Playing Intelligently

It is characteristic of an intelligent person that he doesn't jump into something without first examining his options. At Princeton, I told my players that you cannot intellectualize, you cannot examine fifty alternatives, you cannot resort to committees and subcommittees. You cannot tell me this is a good idea, or how to win a game. You got to Princeton because you learned to use your head, but using your head is only half of life. The heart, the emotions, is something else. If you could solve all your problems by using your head, that's one thing, but you can only solve math problems that way. I remind my players that being intelligent means behaving wisely, with discipline. Too often, an intellectual puts the accent on talking. Playing intelligently means knowing when not to think, too.

■　■　■

No Such Thing as an Ivy League Player

I used to tell my guys: "I know about your academic load. I know how tough it is to give up the time to play here, but let's get one thing straight: In my book, there's no such thing as an Ivy League player. When you come out of that locker room and step across that white line, you are basketball players—period. We play to win, not to say we are an Ivy team and do things differently."

Competing Against a Friend

One of the hardest things to learn is how to compete hard against a friend. Players at any age don't necessarily understand that, but it's especially true at a place like Princeton, where the intensity level of athletics is not what it is at big-time places. What I have noticed lately is that the players don't like to play one-on-one because they think it affects their friendship. Here are two guys walking down to practice. They're good friends. On court, both are trying to play the same spot. How hard do they play each other? As one becomes first string, what will be their relationship? As they leave the practice, will they have the same feeling for each other as they did on the way down? I try to tell them there's a difference between being a friend and being a teammate. A friend is one thing, but a teammate is another. A teammate understands you have to compete, that you want to be better than the other fellow is. The harder they play against each other without being nasty or dirty, or violating the spirit of good competition, the more they learn, and the better friends they'll become because they will respect each other.

That feeling of being competitive should end when you walk back to the dorm.

That is a hard thing for anybody to understand. Players who do not compete hard against each other because they're afraid it will affect their friendship have trouble getting better.

Do Not Come to Princeton to Be Famous

I liked to tell my players that if you came to Princeton to be recognized, you picked the worst place in the world. Here, there are 3,000 kids doing great work every day without any recognition. Just because a guy loves to play basketball doesn't mean the guy who loves to play soccer loves it any less. Everyone loves something and everyone is a star: Someone is working on a combustion engine, or robotics, or nuclear fusion. The students here are all busy—even when they aren't doing anything they're still busy. If your effort matches or exceeds theirs, they will respond. If you're lazy, or not very good, or don't love to play, they won't come to watch your games. A lot of guys don't understand this. If you don't understand it and you want to be treated like a star, Princeton is a bad place. In the end, you try to get the kids to understand that they shouldn't worry about who makes the shot, only whether or not the shot is made.

■ ■ ■

Praise Exposed

Praise is the cheapest form of reward.

Everyone likes to hear he's doing well, and hardly anyone takes criticism the right way, without feeling attacked. I don't like to see a guy get patted on the back for doing simple things, for doing the things he should do. I've given lectures throughout the country, and every time I get fifty coaches coming up to me after the lecture and saying "Nice going" or "Good job" and forty-eight of them didn't mean it. You have to be able to tell a player or a coach when he does a bad job that it is a bad job. I tell my players that if I tell them they played a great game on Tuesday, and on Wednesday I tell them they're messing up, I'm the same coach. You show respect by praising them when they do the things that deserve praise. They must learn the difference between what is done right and what is done wrong, and if you try to make them similar with easy praise you'll never succeed in teaching them the difference.

Over the years when we have won an Ivy title, my players have asked me to get them rings like the football players get, but I've always resisted. My experience with rings is the same as with new cars: After two weeks, you don't notice them anymore, except for a wedding ring—I'd better add that one. Well, we won those four Ivy titles in a row, 1988–92, and I thought I had to do something for my teams so I got them pocket watches to give to their fathers with their son's name inscribed inside and the season's record. Praise, rings, watches—I guess they're nice tokens, but I'd rather have the thing that lasts forever: respect for what you have done. It is important to play the game for the right reasons.

Every Day, a New Day

My motto is that whatever happens on Wednesday, whether you win or lose, whether you have a sense of exhilaration or feel the lowest level of remorse, it has no bearing at all on what happens on Thursday. Every day has to be a new day with a new set of challenges. You forget about wins and near wins over UCLA and Georgetown very quickly. They remain as memories but they cannot affect what goes on the next day. If you shoot 3 for 20, or 17 for 20 on Wednesday, and you try to carry that into Thursday, someone will knock your jock off.

If You Insist on Less, You Get It

My guys say I was rough but that I never lied to them. I am a very demanding coach. Why? You start with the premise that in general people would rather do something less difficult than something difficult. And certain kinds of extreme situations demand high levels of effort. People resist giving that high level of effort. There's a tendency to settle for less and you have to overcome that.

When you demand a lot, my experience has been that you get more. If you insist on less, you get that, too. Nothing brings out a sense of satisfaction better than the successful completion of a difficult task no matter what it is. Self-esteem comes from accomplishment, not the other way around. The more you demand, the more they give, the stronger the sense of satisfaction. You get it from doing anything that's difficult.

I am also a demanding coach because that's how I was

trained. My players might learn something if they ask what era I grew up in. You can't neglect or not notice that life was different when I was growing up: two wars, a poor family, a certain way of behaving compared to now. Today, my players have a proliferation of options. They have so many more choices of things to do that are readily available and that you want to do as opposed to having to do. Growing up in my circumstances there were not that many choices. You generally knew what you had to do. What the hell does that have to do with basketball? A lot. It's the human element in the game. In basketball, there cannot be a proliferation of options and moods and ways of doing things.

That's one of the problems with our education system right now—everybody thinks he or she knows how to run the school system better than the people running it. Maybe you can run a university by committee and let the faculty suggest all their different ideas, but you can't run a basketball team by committee, or have all your players arguing with you all the time about what to do, which choice to make for an offense, or when to practice or what to practice. I mean if you do, what are you going to get?

Speed Wins the Race

My teams often can shoot better, pass better, play better defense, understand better what the game is about, but the opponents are better because they have speed. Someone will teach them the other things, but who can teach my guys speed? Speed follows luck and covers a multitude of sins.

119

Lesson Number One on Offense

There is only one ball. Basketball is a series of one-, two-, and three-man plays; if all five guys were to try to get into the action at the same time they would run into each other. There cannot be competition for the ball. If you have five players competing for the ball, it makes it a lot easier for the defense to guard them.

Get a Good Shot

The main goal of the offense is to get a shot you can make, a good shot, every time you have the ball. The quality of your passing determines the quality of your shots. Bad passing is a limitation on the number of things you can do.

My offense approach is to do something and create options so you have alternatives when the opposing team stops you from doing one thing. We try to create a flow or movement to cover all the possibilities. We learn how to react to various defenses and to take what the defense gives us. Freelance, which is another name for the offense, is hard to teach because the players have to know all the improvisations. A simple pattern offense in which the players learn a few basic maneuvers would be much easier to learn, but even a rat can learn how to run through a maze, and it wouldn't be long before a well-drilled defense would stop a team that depended on such an offense.

Against a man-to-man, the offense must utilize hard cuts toward and away from the ball, down screens and back screens. It seems to me that the faster your team is the more cuts you make, and the slower your team is, the more screens you have to use. We try to get the team to understand that when you're making an offensive move, if you try to help somebody else, when the time comes it is easier to help yourself. If you throw the ball down to the center and he tries to score every time, the defense becomes alerted to that and starts doubling down on the center. Now the center throws the ball back out; that leads to the possibility of a three-point shot, and after a while the defender doubling down on the center is not so eager to do that because he's making it easy for your team to take a three-pointer. So he stops doubling down and the center then starts playing one-on-one with his man again. Our offense at Princeton always tried to make effective use of a center who likes to pass the ball. Our center Kit Mueller got all his points by passing. He didn't have to worry about the defense doubling down on him because the defense had to defend his passing as well—help somebody else, you help yourself.

We mainly try to get the point across that every little thing you do on offense counts. That means that every pass, every cut, every screen, every dribble is part of the end result and therefore requires care and concern. Timing and execution are the keys to everything we try to do. We try to make it simple and we work hard to make things easy.

Closing the Talent Gap

Against a run-and-shoot team with more talent and speed than your team, you want to make the game a shorter contest in order to close the gap between their talent and

121

yours. You don't want to take the first good shot you get, but wait for the third or fourth good shot. We played North Carolina A&T in the preliminary round of the NCAA in 1983, were outrebounded 67 to 25, and won 53–41. They played Ping-Pong with the ball, throwing the ball up six, seven, eight times to make one basket. We played deliberately, waiting for good shots, and then making them. You are never in trouble as long as you have the ball. In the first round of the 1976 NCAA, we played an undefeated Rutgers. Again, we played deliberately—it was before the shot clock—and almost won, coming back from eight down at the half to lose by one, 54–53. Of course, sometimes it backfires. Earlier that same year, we played Rutgers at Princeton and had the ball, down by two, with four or five minutes to go. Armond Hill got his fourth foul and had to come out so I froze the ball for two minutes to make the game shorter until we could get him back in. But at the two-minute mark, Rutgers stole the ball and scored and eventually won 75–62.

Play Without the Ball (and the Coach)

We do have some set plays, but we try to teach all the possibilities that can come from any one play: The fundamental teaching point here is to watch your teammate in front of you. He will tell you what you should do by what he himself does. He might cut to get open, or cut to free an area—to make it open for someone else to go in there. Or he might go to help someone else by setting a screen. These are the three things that he or you can do without the ball. All four guys

122

who don't have the ball have to have an idea of what to do. They have to play without the ball—keep their defensive men moving, divert them, get them to turn their head. If your teammate, instead of cutting through, sets a screen, you could come off that screen. Or if your defender is playing you close, you might go back-door. You will know what to do by watching the man in front of you. It's a fundamental tenet that applies to every offense that I know of.

Two further points: I do not like to have my players cut and go behind the man with the ball. It leads to trouble. I like them to go away from the ball. Secondly, if you watch your teammate with the ball pass it and then cut to the basket, you must know that you cannot cut the same way he did. If you do, then the man who now has the ball has no one left to play with.

You can play without a coach if you understand this principle. I had a situation once, against Virginia down at Charlottesville, where I thought the referees were awful and I got tossed from the game with twenty minutes left. My assistant coaches were all off scouting, so I was alone that night. I told one of my players, Peter Molloy, to take over and run the team while I watched from a distance. He did and we won 55–50. It confirmed what I believe: that you can play without a coach if you understand the basic principles of our offense. Compare it to a system where you have to run exactly where the coach tells you in a set routine or pattern. It's restrictive and, generally speaking, easy to defend.

That game provided me with the most satisfaction of any game that I've ever been in, because it showed me that my teaching had taken effect, that they could play and know what to do without me and win. Incidentally, that team also won the NIT at the end of the season.

Cut with Credibility

What I like my guys to do on offense to start a game is pass and cut through the defense. The minute you do, you start to move the defense, a main goal. The main reason to cut, of course, is to get open to receive a pass, or to clear an area and help set up something for a teammate. It also helps to identify the defense, whether it's a zone, a combo, or a man-to-man.

Most of the time, the defender has already established his position relative to yours, which makes it easier for you to cut. If he is contesting your movement, you will probably cut behind him. If he is playing loosely, you will probably cut in front and toward the ball. You step one way and cut back the other—in other words, fake going one way and cut back another. The cut should be crisp and hard. You don't run right at your defender, unless you do it to make him move, or to intimidate him. Most of the time, your defender will tell you which direction to cut by how he moves. If he tries not to let you cut—he is playing denial defense, or overplaying you—then cut behind him. This cut as we know is called a backdoor, or a give-and-go.

It is essential that when the cutter cuts through, he look for the ball. There will be no credibility to the cut unless the player executes it with authenticity, i.e., believes he might receive the ball and therefore runs to get open, or to set something up for a teammate. This is another example of how each guy, when he does something to help his teammate, helps himself. When you pass to the open man, you make everybody's cut more credible, and when the cuts are credible there are more open men to pass to. If someone doesn't cut hard, it's because he doesn't believe he will get the ball, or he doesn't care enough. Remember, he has to watch where he's cutting; if the ball doesn't come, he runs away from the ball —somewhere where he's not going to get in the way of the next sequence that's going to happen on offense.

Back-Door

If two players are going to play together, each has to be involved, either by one passing to the other or by dribbling over to him. Any other way is a violation. That is the only way they can play together and that's the beginning of team play. If you're the dribbler and your teammate is open, throw it to him. That starts the offense. But what if you can't throw it to him because he's covered? You start dribbling toward him. He sees you dribbling toward him and reacts to how his defender is guarding him. We want him to fake a step in one direction, then turn sharply on an angle that forms a V and cut behind the defender, looking for a pass from his teammate. In other words, the open man goes in the back door of the defense to the basket.

When you're guarded so closely that you aren't free to catch a pass, it means the defender is playing denial defense—he has turned his back partially to the ball. That's when you want to go back-door. The defender can't watch the ball out front and you cutting behind him at the same time. Years ago, the back-door play was called "change of direction." A player going one way suddenly cut in a different direction. It doesn't sound as nice, so, today we call it the back-door. Regardless, we made a living out of that play at Princeton. We have had as many as fifty back-doors in a single game. Against North

Carolina one year, we had twenty-five back-doors—they over-played us, and we had the kind of passing and cutting that are essential to play against a tight defense.

Generally speaking, a player will pass the ball to his team-mate when he is open. Sometimes I will ask the passer, "Why didn't you throw it to that guy?" and he'll say " 'Cause he wasn't open" and I'll say, "That's right." That's when you drib-ble over to him. When you can't throw it, take it over to him. It should be obvious. If you can't take it to him, or throw it to him, it's because he is being closely guarded. So when you move toward him with the ball, and you don't throw it to him because you see that he is guarded, he knows what to do because you did not throw him the ball in the first place: He steps or fakes toward you and cuts back-door.

I generally don't like to have players who are closely guarded move toward the man with the ball because it leads to trouble. When you run over to the dribbler, you take the defender with you. That makes it impossible for the dribbler to do anything by himself and to do anything to help you. But when you run away from the ball, when you cut hard back-door, that puts your defender on alert that you know how to play without the ball. That's the irony of the whole play: that by going back-door and scoring, you make the defense aware that you can do that. As a result, when you come out front for the ball next time, the defender has to loosen up and be alert for your back-door cut. That now makes it more possible for you to receive the ball out in front again and shoot because the defender is a little afraid to overplay you.

It takes a while to teach the back-door. Almost instinctively, the player without the ball wants to go toward the ball. Why not? That's how he's been trained to get the ball, and, of course, he wants to shoot—that's why they put the hoop

126

up there; no one would play this game if they took the basket down. Some players want to shoot so badly they follow the ball everywhere—I kid them about having some radar connection between them and the ball. They have to learn to play without the ball. For that reason, a lot of guys don't like to do the back-door. It may be a little simple, or they just don't see it.

A lot of players cannot play without the ball. They don't know what to do when they don't have the ball: They don't know how or where to cut, or how to set a screen, or how to make themselves useful to the rest of the team. There are a lot of players like that and what they do is smother the team. They perform very well for themselves. So many people are geared to following the ball and you have to change their mind-set. But you can. I have kids at my summer camps who, after two days, know how to play without the ball. They're willing to learn.

We have a back-door off the low post that involves the center. We create the back-door from a dribble screen. The possibilities flow one from the other and we work on them until they become natural: The player comes around and goes in for a layup, or he comes around and stops behind a screen, or he drives the opposite way, or he passes and goes back-door for a return pass—all of these are possibilities when two players come together, and we work on them over and over, first without a defender, then we put a defender in there to guard the dribbler, then to guard the guy who is going to get the pass. We work on getting each player to see what the other is doing and going to do, to see what's available. Each player must look at what he is doing and where he is going, and what the others are doing and where they are going.

In general, teams that go back-door well are teams that

127

shoot well, because defenses work harder against good-shooting teams. That follows, because what makes the back-door possible is a defense that guards your players closely to try to stop them from shooting. The defense that has a tendency to overplay their opponents opens up areas for cutting and passing back-door. Chuck Daly, when he coached at Penn, would seldom overplay us because of the back-door. Some teams play us so hard to stop the back-door, as if that's all we have. Others pack it in there and we cannot do it, but then we come around for the ball and take the easy shots out front. If you have a bad-shooting team, that makes it rough. Again, you look at the defense—what is there? The vernacular —it comes from football—is to do what the defense gives you. You have to prepare your team for whatever the situation calls for. That's the fundamental goal of your teaching. If you do that and have some talent to coach, you're going to have some success.

Our Offense Simplified

I used to go to Andy's Tavern in Princeton, and I went there once the night before I was supposed to do a clinic. Sitting at the bar were some friends of mine named Whisky Steve, Potato Mike, Little Joe, and Uncle Joe, who owned the place. When I walked in, all the guys said "Hi coach," and I said, "Hey, fellas, I'm going to a clinic tomorrow in St. Louis and I have to give a lecture on offense. Do you have any ideas?" Whisky Steve, who was half in the bag, looks at me and says with a slur, "Tell 'em to watch where they're going."

That's it—that's the basis of our offense. The players have to know and watch. You plan to do something and you create options so you have alternatives when the opposing team stops you from doing one thing. We try to create a flow or movement to cover all the possibilities. The challenge is to retain the opportunity for creativity, the capability to react and take advantage of new options. The players have to know all the improvisations.

Whisky Steve and the others gave me four or five more ideas and I refined them and used them at the clinic the next day, and the coaches wanted to buy them from me at two dollars a sheet. I will never forget that.

Who Is Doing It?

No matter what, the most important thing is who is doing it. You can make almost anything work if the right guy is doing it. Take a player like Frank Sowinski ('78); he could go over the top of a double screen and intercept passes, or get out to the corner to pick up a guy there, but he always had trouble keeping his body in front of the man he was guarding if the guy had the ball. Now you take Bobby Slaughter on the same team, another great player, who was faster than Frank but he couldn't get out to the corner and do what Frank could. But try to drive on Bobby—whoa, that was dangerous. He stole half the balls and always cut you off. So one guy was faster in one thing and slower in the other—little things that a coach has to notice to be sure he has the right guy doing what he wants done.

Good Reading Habits

Our disciplined offense was based on the great Boston Celtic teams of the 1950s and '60s. I loved watching the Celtics play. They were so good at what they did. I loved the way Bob Cousy handled the ball and Bill Russell played the post. To absorb all of this, I've always done three things as a coach: watched, listened, and read. Unfortunately, I was not—and still am not—a good reader. The way I learned best was by watching and listening. It gave me great insight into the game and into my profession. Many times, my assistant coaches and I would sit down and discuss what happened in the game the night before. It is incredible the things that happen that are not seen.

Pay Attention

When I was a kid, I had some kind of eye problem that was never corrected—we were a poor family and I don't think I ever realized, or my parents didn't, that I had a problem that might have been corrected at an early age. I had a tendency to see double lines and words. As a result, while I've never had any trouble shooting a basketball, it has always been hard for me to read—I never let that stop me, but it's been hard. To compensate for that, I learned early on to pay attention. I am very good at paying attention. When I'm watching a game, I really watch it, whether it's my own team, or a pro game, or a high school game where I'm looking at a possible prospect. I don't notice what's going on around me, and people who try to talk to me at games give up. The point is I am paying attention, and it's unbelievable what you can see and learn when you do.

Bounce Passes on the Back-Door

We like to throw bounce passes off the dribble on our back-door plays. I tell the guys to pass off the dribble because if you pick up the ball, the defender who's guarding you sees you, thinks pass, and sticks his hands where you're going to throw it. But if you don't pick up the ball, the defender can't tell whether you're going to continue to dribble, or pass.

The pass off the dribble is just a little push. You don't have to wind up. We tell the passer to aim for the rear end of the defender. When the defender sees his man cut back-door, sometimes he reverse-pivots to face the passer. Although it is hard for the defender to get his hand on the ball if he's starting with his back to the passer, by reverse pivoting he can get his hands into the path of the ball if the passer isn't careful. The way I teach it, you aim the pass for the rear of the defender so that when he turns or opens to the ball, which is what most coaches teach, it's too late and your guy already has the ball. The bounce pass works well in close quarters because it makes the defender have to bend over to stop it. But when you try to throw a bounce pass any distance, the second it hits the floor it becomes an awfully slow pass. We practiced this pass hard and we were pretty successful at it.

■ ■ ■

Slower Fast Break

Most of my teams at Princeton were opportunity fast break teams. We didn't have many burners in the last decade or so—the ability to get guys downcourt. We didn't have the picture fast breaks. Since we weren't able to run that well, we had to play a lot of half-court. People thought our deliberate style of play was because we played slow-down offense, but it was as much because we contested every pass and shot.

The fast break is so nice to see—besides the excitement of it, which the fans love, it's also a form of precision basketball. But if the game of basketball gets to a stage where there's no mental side to it—where it's all run and shoot and physical violence—it won't last. You can't get the pros and certain colleges to slow down. But if you look at basketball during the last four years or so, the Final Fours and the NBA playoffs, there's been a lot more half-court and conservative play.

Small, Slow Shooters

We had small, slow but excellent shooters, hardly ever rebounded, but we won more than 70 percent of our games because our skill level was high and we could do things to compensate for our lack of speed.

When a player is slow, the defender will not pay as close attention to him and you get an imbalance. But continuous offensive movement of the ball lets slower guys play. The slow guy can use the flow of the offense to get open, to shoot, to cut, to make a pass. If a player is slow, he has to have a high skill level to compete.

The Three-Point Shot

I love the three-point shot. You know why? Because it means they're giving us three points for the same shot we used to get two for.

Driving Is a Knack

I've heard this attributed to John Wooden at UCLA: There is a knack to being a good rebounder. I've analyzed that down through the years and I agree. It seems as though there is a knack to almost anything you do on the court. Driving around your man, for example, takes a certain knack. It might be that the guy has a great first step or whatever—it doesn't matter, he can get by his man, whereas someone who might be faster or quicker or a better athlete doesn't seem to beat his man. He doesn't have the knack. A stand-still shooter can only make shots when he is standing still; when you crowd him, he won't drive—he has no knack for driving.

Knack for Rebounding

Certain guys like Dennis Rodman for Chicago always seem to find a way to get the rebound. Bill Russell said that 60 percent of rebounding during a game occurs below the level of the rim, which puts a premium on the strategy of boxing out. I'm not sure about the accuracy of Russell's theory

133

today, especially when you look at all the guys who are being recruited because they can jump over the rim.

I've had a few players here who have had the knack, but for the most part two staples of basketball, leaping ability and speed, have not been staples at Princeton. We were outrebounded just about every year I was there. Sometimes I think it was my fault because I didn't stress it enough. Other times, I think there were factors that had little relevance to getting the ball, or what I was doing. When I first came, I was so worried about compensating for our inadequate rebounding that I was really on my guys in practice about it, but instead of getting better we seemed to get worse. One of my players finally came to me and said I was making them nervous, so I slacked off.

Given the rebounding situation at Princeton, you would think I'd have put a premium on boxing out, the way most coaches do. I've always felt that boxing out is easy to do. It basically involves two things: One is to remember to do it enough so that it becomes a habit. That's easy enough to understand because the obvious instinct is to go for the ball and forget about the man. Nothing is worse than watching a guy so intent on boxing out his man that he stops watching the ball and it bounces off his head.

Then there is a second problem: When you box out a player, it makes it hard for you to get the rebound. You can get trapped so that you can't move. Boxing out is not a bad idea if you see that it enables your own teammate to get the ball, but when you box out your man, make sure you don't box yourself out. Teams that box out well are rough to play against because you've always got your belly bumping into a guy's back. Still, I think the best way to get the ball is to go after it.

134

Who Gets the Rebound?

Size is not the most important thing about rebounding. Knowing how to use your body, seeing where the ball is going, that's what counts. Dave Debusschere of the Knicks was a great rebounder; Larry Bird, too. It is not the guy who jumps the highest. The guy who jumps the highest gets the ball when he is all alone. Jumping in a crowd, that's another story. Just watch guys like Bird. It is a lesson. A good rebounder plays for position, but is always attentive to the ball. You cannot lose sight of the ball. You've got to have some idea where the ball is going and how to prevent your man from getting it.

Where's the Nearest Railroad?

A player's ability to rebound is inversely proportional to the distance between where he was born and the nearest railroad tracks. Or, the greater the distance you live from the poor side of the railroad tracks, the less likely it is that you'll be a good rebounder. There are certain parts of this game where you can get hurt, and rebounding is one of them. One of the challenges of rebounding is not being afraid to rebound. The game is very physical underneath the boards, more today than ever before. It's violent, and if you're afraid of a loose elbow breaking your nose or jaw, you will not do anything.

What I have noticed is that guys who don't come from houses with three-car garages seem to have a desire to get in there under the boards and get smacked. If you have the technique for boxing a guy out, but when you go to do it you're afraid that he's going to kill you, you aren't going to get the ball. That was one of Larry Bird's greatest assets. He went in there in a crowd, and he was not afraid. He was fearless.

Hands Don't Change

You cannot do much for a player's hands. I've heard all kinds of things for trying to teach a player to hold on to the ball: "Look the ball into your hands"—all that stuff. I've found that some athletes improve and some continue to drop balls. I had a guy here who dropped seven out of eight passes but would never drop a rebound. You explain that one. Twelve years after he left here, this fellow came back for an alumni game. As soon as he came running onto the court, someone threw him the ball. It went right through his hands again. He was still the same.

Solving a Press

My Princeton teams were always pressed a lot. That's because when you're slow, you get pressed. But, we weren't pressed successfully too often. That's because in recruiting, I looked for guys who could pass and for ball handlers. Billy Ryan ('84) beat the press over and over with just one pass— he could always find the open man. When I had George Left-wich ('92), nobody pressed us for four years. Nowadays, there is a shortage of passers—hardly any one passes that well. I don't know why players are not passing better except that I think it has to do with the age of specialization.

When you get pressed, there are three important things you need: First, you need someone who is good at taking the ball out—someone who can see which man is open and isn't going to get into trouble if he gets the ball. If the guy throwing the ball in panics, or is blind, he's going to throw the ball hurriedly, and because of where he throws it he's going to get the player catching it in trouble.

Second, you need a player who can advance the ball to the other end of the court. Billy Omeltchenko ('78) always looked like the kind of guy every defender thought he could steal the dribble from. He'd get surrounded by defensive guys and they'd be licking their chops while he struggled to get free, and then all of a sudden he would whip that ball to the open guy for the pass that led to a layup. He always seemed able to wiggle out of trouble and find the open man. (Another example of an intangible.) You try not to throw the ball to a player who doesn't see his teammates.

Third, you have to have a scorer at the end of the press, someone who knows what to do when he gets the ball. When you can convert a press into a score for yourself, then the psychology of the press changes in your favor—the other team doesn't want to press you because they know you will kill them.

Inbounds Passes

When we had to throw the ball in against a press, we would often have the inbounder make the initial pass to a teammate who had stepped out of bounds as well. We used this especially against a 1-2-1-1 press where the defense had put a man on our inbounder so he couldn't see up the court. Instead, he would throw to his teammate, who by stepping out of bounds no longer had anyone in front of him. He now could look upcourt and find the open man to throw to. That strategy is predicated on having two good inbounds passers. It also helps to keep the ball out of the corners where the defense can trap you. This worked very well for us. It also forced the opponents to match up thereby defining the press better for us.

Jump Balls

Taking away the jump ball didn't really hurt a team like Princeton since we didn't have players tall enough to control the tap. One good thing was that we didn't have to worry about that anymore, and we didn't have to spend all that practice time preparing for them. I just told my players not to give up a layup. On the other hand, its elimination is a further example of the decline of what I call the cerebral nature of the game of basketball. If there is anything I worry about, it's that the rush to make the game more entertaining will end up taking the cerebral element out of it.

When I was a coach at Reading High School, you had six, seven, maybe more jump balls a game and you had to be concerned about how you would play if the other team got the tap. You had to consider and practice different strategies: Did you go for the steal, and how did you protect your basket? One year, we played the number one team in the state at the start of the season and they beat us handily. I tried to find something good to tell my team after the game and discovered we'd won most of the jump balls, maybe eight or nine. I told them that was going to pay off someday. We played the same team again in the playoffs at the end of the season and with seventeen seconds to go, we were ahead by one point and there was a jump ball underneath their basket. We stole the tap and ran out the clock to win.

There are only two jump balls in a game now—one to start the game, and one to start an overtime. Otherwise, you have alternating possessions as a replacement for the jump ball. The rule was changed on the grounds that the referees were not good at throwing up the ball. I always thought that was a foolish explanation, and not very honest. First, it's faulty reasoning to say a referee cannot throw the ball up right so let's eliminate the need for him to do that. Thomas Jefferson used the term "education of discretion" to mean that if somebody does not know how to do something, teach him how to do it instead of taking away his opportunity to do it. No, the real reason for eliminating the jump ball was to speed up the game—and that's what they should have said.

Cerebral Basketball

When you take out the cerebral part of the game, you remove the part that enabled a player with limited ability but a head for the game to contribute. And when you limit the ability of a player to develop in a fundamentally sound way by teaching him only a specialized role, you limit his ability to use his head. He cannot take advantage of the different opportunities he sees because his skills are limited. A coach who has to teach a player or a team that is lacking in fundamentals finds his options limited and winds up with a highly restricted and structured offense. It's a good example of a self-fulfilling prophecy.

You could not find a better example of a nonrestrictive offense based on a high skill level than that of the Chicago Bulls, the champions of professional basketball. The Bulls don't care who they throw the ball to because they can all pass, three are expert dribblers, two can dribble enough to get the job done, and they're all decent shooters. The result is the most flowing type of offense you can have. And look at their ratings on television. Indiana, Duke, North Carolina—they also move the ball, pass, play defense; they are exponents of the cerebral aspects of the game. To play a cerebral game, you need a high level of skill.

There are not that many people anymore who care about the lost cerebral aspects of the game. There are only a few who seem to appreciate a crafty team trying to set up the other team, like a crafty pitcher in baseball: Sal Maglie of the old New York Giants, or Whitey Ford of the New York Yankees back in the 1950s. Compare them to the fireballer, the guy who throws it in there past the batters. Which do you want? What the fans want shows up on the court, in every sport. Because sooner or later, what the fans want gets translated into what the players want. The players want to be successful.

■ ■ ■

Make a Zone Run

First, you must recognize the zone: Is it a 2-1-2, 2-3, 1-2-2, 1-3-1, or some combination? Then you must remember that your decision how to attack the zone has to be based on the shot you can make. To say it another way: The shot you can make dictates your offense against any zone. The goal is to get an uncontested shot, or a shot with a good opportunity to get fouled.

The quality of your passing will determine the quality of your shot. To me, nothing makes attacking a zone more difficult than bad passing. Bad passing limits the kinds of things you try to do.

Try to put your man in between any two of theirs. When you throw a pass, there should not be anyone in front of you. When you catch the pass, there should not be anyone in front of you either. If either situation is negative, then you're in the wrong place and haven't recognized the zone.

Try to make as many cuts as you can from behind the zone. When you cut in front, the defense can see you and that makes it easier to defend against what you're trying to do.

Move the ball and move yourself so that you make the zone "run." That takes the zone out of its shape, or makes the slides longer and more difficult to do.

If you're going to penetrate or drive through the zone, try not to stop in between two of their men, but rather go past them.

Teach your team the slides used by the defense in the zone. Because if the other coach knows something about his zone, you can know the same thing, too.

If you aren't going to beat the zone by fast breaking, then develop good patience and put the zone to work for you.

One Gym Versus Another

The only bad part about playing in Jadwin as opposed to the old Dillon Gym, which is located in the center of campus, was that I didn't get to see the players during the course of the day, since Jadwin is at the edge of the campus. When there was only Dillon Gym, the players would walk by the office during the day, and I could yell out the window at them.

Turn on the Fans

I love a good crowd. I always felt, and I told this to my players, that at certain schools, the fans turn on the kids, but at this school you have to turn on the fans. They will not accept a slovenly effort, or players who don't care. But they will root for guys who work hard. Through your effort and intelligence, you get people into the gym. Lots of Princeton fans and Ivy Leaguers in general don't seem very vocal at first, but all of a sudden, they recognize what you're doing and they become part of it. If you take a look at our win over North Carolina (89–73) in the 1971–72 season, our fans were running through our field house afterward yelling "We did it! We did it!" You have to excite the fans at Princeton.

People always talk about the crowd being a sixth man, an advantage. I always told my guys that when you play and the crowd is hostile, use that and it will make you work harder. Once we were playing on our own court, against Yale, and Jadwin was empty. We had just completed two championship seasons in succession, but that year we were not so hot and the fans deserted us. Just before halftime we were playing for the last shot, and some guy in our band blew a horn and my guy thought it was the shot clock and threw up a shot and missed. I told my team at halftime that there are guys out there rooting against you. You gotta get mad, and they did and we won. Another time, in 1995, we were honoring the 1975 NIT championship team at halftime against Dartmouth. We were down by 11. As the NIT team comes on the floor to be introduced, one of our fans yelled "Suit 'em up!" I used that comment in the locker room, telling the players there was extra pressure to win because our fans did not support them. We won in the second half and we turned on the fans with some beautiful back-door cuts.

The fans were a factor for us in the Penn playoff game last year up at Lehigh. They came in numbers and they cheered constantly. When we beat Loyola Marymount, Jadwin seats 7,500 but there was a crowd of 8,000 and they started showing up at eleven for a two o'clock game. They had painted their faces and were wearing T-shirts with logos and "deee-fense" painted on them. After the game, they poured onto the floor by the thousands, which you hardly ever see. They behaved like the famous sixth man. That Loyola team was the antithesis of Princeton basketball. It had a fast break offense and they played by number: the five guy took the ball out of bounds and threw to the one man, while two and three ran down the sidelines. We doubled the number one man so they could not throw the inbounds pass to him. They threw instead to the four man, who was not downcourt and who was not as good a ball handler as their one man. We pressed them when four got the ball and slowed their attack and that was pretty much the end of that.

Every year, I make fan support the subject of one of my pregame talks. I tell the team they have to play basketball for the right reasons, which are to be good at what they're doing, show teamwork, and of course win, and that whether someone is there to watch them or not is irrelevant. All you ever want out of any away game is a fair shake from the refs. A hostile crowd, a different backboard or gym floor, whatever—that stuff really should not affect who wins or loses.

Princeton-Penn

My doctor in Philadelphia is a Cornell graduate and he goes to see every Penn-Princeton game at the Palestra and sends me a letter after each game telling me that the five dollars for the ticket was the best money he ever spent. When a stranger not connected to either team makes a remark like that, that just demonstrates that it's a rivalry with few parallels in basketball. In my twenty-nine years at Princeton, Penn or Princeton won the Ivy title every year but three. One year we beat Penn at the Palestra by one point. Dick Kuchen, the Yale coach, went home and told his staff that he had never in his life seen anything like the intensity he witnessed in that game by both teams—and he had coached at Notre Dame and at California in the Pac-10.

Penn has won more Ivy titles than we have and was a basketball power before Princeton. The history of the sport at Penn can be traced through the Palestra, which in the minds of many people is one of the greatest arenas in the country for basketball. We've had some great games there, with Penn, with Temple, St. Joseph's, Villanova, La Salle—we played every Big Five team there at least once. It's a nice place to play and I played there in high school in 1948. We played

Palmerton High School, who were led by a player named Bill Mlkvy, who went on to Temple where he became known as the "Owl without the vowel." My high school coach thought the water in Philadelphia was bad so he brought bottled water down from Bethlehem for us to drink at that game.

The Princeton-Penn game is a reflection of differences between the two schools. The administration at Penn has always paid particular attention to basketball and football, while at Princeton the philosophy has been to try to be good at every sport. That's not to say that Princeton's way is better; it's just a different approach. But no sport in the Ivies attracts the kind of national attention that basketball does. When Princeton beat UCLA last year, we got national and international acclaim—clips from Hong Kong, Spain, all over Europe.

There's also a distinct difference between Penn fans and Princeton fans. Princeton fans get up for the Penn game, but Penn fans love their team; they follow them everywhere and root like hell. You hear the Penn fans yell "Prep school! Prep school!" and the Princeton fans yell back "High school! High school!" It's pretty funny and pretty interesting. The Penn fans were a little rough on me. I was viewed as the ogre who prevented them from having the success they deserved. They devoted one entire halftime show at a football game to doing a satire of me; I didn't take it personally, but I also didn't think it was funny. I was sitting there thinking, "What the hell is going on—this is a football game and what the hell does this have to do with football?" But for the most part I respected their behavior. I can remember one year when Penn was 2-10 and ready to fall apart as they prepared for a game against Penn State, led by a former coach of theirs, Dick Harter. Penn fans turned out for that game in droves and provided such a lift for that team that it beat Penn State and went on to win the Ivy title.

Princeton's games with Penn are very physical. At the Palestra, there's always the feeling that Princeton teams can be intimidated—it's the prep school image, and the fact that we had very few physical teams. I didn't feel in my heart of hearts that we could be intimidated, and the fact that that feeling might exist among Penn players and fans just provided us with more motivation. We've beaten Penn by as much as 25 points down there. They feel they can jump on our backs, get a lot of offensive rebounds, play tough defense. Penn has never surprised us and we've never surprised them. It's a game that has always been played in the trenches. And you cannot underrate their players or their coaches—several have gone onto the pros.

I think as a program it's a little better than ours was, which I've admitted on several occasions. There have been accusations down through the years about recruiting and admission practices at Penn, questions about Penn's standards for athletes, whether they were lower than those for the rest of the league. My comment on that is that each school has its own way of doing what it needs to do, its own mission, its own sense of economy. Whatever Penn does is its own business and only should be noticed and mentioned when there's a violation of the rules. The rest of it is just crap.

■ ■ ■

The Real Stars at Princeton

The real superstars there are in the library. In fact, some of them take their sleeping bags into the stacks so they can study off and on all night long.

Winning

I remember telling my friends after I had been at Princeton a few years: "I'm entering the last third of my life. I have done a reasonable job. My son works hard, my daughter, too. I cannot envision being sick or old. Right now, right or wrong, what I worry about most is being good at what I am doing. I would not know how to behave if we started losing." I don't know where or how it started, but most certainly, my coaches in high school and college helped to instill the ethos, and the great coaches I've coached against have also stressed it: It is important to do things right and it is equally important to be good at what you are doing.

Pick

There are two kinds of picks: The screen is either set by the man with the ball or for the man with the ball. When the player who sets the screen does not have the ball, I consider that mostly a one-on-one play, since the guy without the ball cannot do anything except pick. Once he's set the pick, he can roll to the basket—one of the oldest plays in the game.

It had disappeared from the game of basketball at the college level for about twenty years and then it returned about five years ago, and now there are lots of teams who use it and that's all they do. In the NBA films I see, the pick-and-roll is everywhere and nobody seems able to do much about it there, either, because of league rules restricting different team defensive concepts.

Then there is the pick by the man who has the ball, which is a dribble screen. That's a two-man play that you use when your teammate is closely guarded and you can't pass to him. Most of the time, your teammate should go back door, but if the defender drops off your teammate, you dribble toward him and he comes toward you in such a way that you move between him and the man guarding him. You pick up the dribble and hand it off to him, then try to screen the defender, or cut behind him and run back-door. It is both a horizontal and vertical screen. This is the start of two-on-two basketball with a dribble. I personally think it's harder to defend than the standard pick-and-roll.

Now, why pick? You pick so that someone gets a free shot. A free shot comes when you have the time to shoot without anyone disturbing it. Since my Princeton teams got slower through the years, we picked and screened a lot. As a result, my teams had a lot of free shots. Very few teams ever stopped us from getting free shots.

Some players are more adept at creating their own shot. Be careful to notice that, because sometimes a pick or a screen can get in the way of what your teammate is trying to do—you're trying to help, but you're getting in the way of his success.

■　■　■

Pivoting

Pivoting is one of the most underrated techniques and skills, and when you go to teach it, someone always asks, "Why bother?" We have to teach the player to disregard the feeling that it's not essential, that it's not necessary in today's game. One reason some players disregard its importance is that they do it so easily. The pivot is also an important and effective move for the defender.

If you can pivot sharply, it gives you another way, maybe the only way, to get by a defender, or to get yourself out of a trap that you're gotten into. Say you drive hard for the basket but get cut off. You then have the option of pivoting away from the defender with either foot. You pivot and get your back into the defender so there is contact. You immobilize his body. You feel where he is, then roll off his body in either direction. In a sense, you use his body to score.

Thirty or forty years ago, a player would not turn his back on his man because it was thought it would invite trouble—a double team or a trap. I used to tell my guys they could do anything just as long as they didn't turn their backs. Earl Monroe became so clever at pivoting as a technique for getting by his man that it added a whole new opportunity for guys who couldn't otherwise get by their defender. Today, people are so good at pivoting and finding the open man if the defense tries to double up or trap him. I recall once watching Jimmy Lynam, coach of the Washington Bullets, at a clinic demonstrating pivoting. He had five players on the floor trying to trap him, and just by pivoting he got free of every mess.

Generally, guys with large feet seem to have more trouble pivoting smoothly. It's like they pivot by the numbers: toe first, then the sole, then the heel. Maybe it's because big feet can be harder to maneuver. You have to turn the whole foot around in a complete turn. It's even harder to do with the ball.

Fakes Are Like Lies

The first thing I tell anyone about faking is that if you're going to fake, your move has to look like the real thing. When you go to tell a lie, it has to be close enough to the truth to be believable. Same thing. So often, guys fake so strenuously that they telegraph the fake: Their fake looks like a fake. When you fake a shot, if you stare up in the air and give a hard jerk of your arms, if that isn't what you normally do when you shoot, you won't fool anyone. And if you fake a shot but the defense knows you can't shoot, no one will fall for the fake. Also, if you're wide open, don't fake—shoot!

Some guys fake by instinct and move the defense. Young kids have to be actors and develop cunning. They shouldn't work only on one fake; you always want to have more than one weapon.

Faking isn't something that only the offense does. The defense can fake, too. A fast defender who is adept at stealing passes can slack off his man, pretend to be beaten, and when the passer throws it to his man, he suddenly steps in and steals the pass.

■ ■ ■

Preseason Stuff

Many players spend time running and lifting weights in the preseason to get in shape. I've never been a stickler for that stuff. It can help, but I don't think that's the best way to get into shape, or to improve your basketball skills. You can get stronger, faster, and more agile by playing the game. Also, both player and coach have to recognize that playing in the preseason without a coach has limited value in improving your skills. It's more a time for the guys to develop team camaraderie; they can get to know each other and enjoy each other without a coach around.

Conditioning

I tell my players if you play hard every time you play, you'll be in good enough shape—as a matter of fact, you'll never have to worry about getting tired. I had some players who came to Princeton having gotten their ideas about conditioning from coaches who took a scientific approach to the subject. There's nothing particularly wrong about that, but five days into the season they seemed to get hurt. I'd get an occasional player who says he's been working all summer with So-and-So on a certain physiological approach to conditioning, and he'd run up and down the court twice and get pooped. You can see I have some disdain for modern technology. There is no substitute for playing hard.

My high school coach was great for conditioning. I was always down at the Boys Club at night after practice playing pickup games. One year we had to play a big game against

Hazleton, a power in Eastern Pennsylvania high school basketball. The day before the game, we finish practice and the coach makes me promise not to play that night. So I tell him don't worry, and my friend Rocco and I go to the club to play pool. A bunch of fellows come in looking for two more guys to play some ball. We can't play because we have a big game tomorrow. Well, okay, we'll just play one game. We played till midnight. We go up to Hazleton and press them all over the court and beat them. Their coach said after the game that I had put on such a show he was nominating me for all-state. My coach told me he appreciated the fact that I hadn't gone down to the Club, that the team had needed my energy. All the while he's telling me this, I can see in his face that he knows.

I've noticed within my own teams that guys who love to play and play a lot don't seem to get hurt. I've also noticed over the years that we seemed to have fewer injuries as a team than a lot of our competitors. I remember watching some pro teams come to Princeton to train in the preseason. I would watch their daily practices, watch them condition and stretch, but a bunch of them were hurt—a pulled this, a sore that, and these guys are supposed to be in tip-top shape. I really believe that if you play as hard as you can all the time you're playing, you'll never get out of shape. But never say never: Reggie Bird hardly played preseason with the other guys, and then on the first day of practice he would run everybody into the ground and he would keep on running the rest of the season. More typical was Kevin "Moon" Mullins ('84), whom I recruited away from Haverford. I saw him score 50 points in a game but I wasn't sure I wanted him. He didn't look that strong, he played in a lousy league, and he seemed more likely to play tennis somewhere. He turned out to be a fourth-round draft pick in the NBA. His first two years at Princeton, he would get tired and make mistakes. In his sophomore year, he played my assistant Mickey Steurer, who had graduated eight years earlier, one-on-one. First game, Mickey won 7–6. The second game, Mickey won 7–3, and the third, Mickey won 7–0. Mullins was so tired he needed a backstop to hold him up. He decided he had had enough of being tired. Next thing I heard Moon was running everywhere he went on campus, to class, to the gym, everywhere. He was running like a man possessed. And when he showed up for the new season, he kept on running. In the NCAA tournament that year, he scored 39 against San Diego and 23 against Las Vegas. If he'd been shooting well against Vegas, he'd have had 50 because they couldn't stop him. He was the last guy cut in the pros— if he'd had some experience as a guard instead of a forward, he might have made it.

Once practice starts, we work hard and that's the best conditioning there is. Everything counts. Every little thing counts. Run hard, play hard, go after the ball hard, guard hard. If you play soft—what I call a "nonaggression pact" with your teammates—you won't ever get in shape. Everything we do is game-condition because how you play in practice is how you'll play in a game.

Weight-Training

My guys do off-season weights. I believe weights can help improve strength and stamina, but I never really institutionalized lifting until very recently. I used to say it was up to the players but then some guys wouldn't do it, or wouldn't do

153

it very much. My assistant coaches told me we should insist that the entire team do it, and so that's what we told them, and we got better results. You have to do it during the season, too; if you stop lifting, you lose the strength you've gained in about two weeks of a normal season.

"And Two's"

I have a little running game that I used a lot called "And two's." It's really a passing drill, and a fun drill: You run upcourt, passing back and forth, then you shoot a layup. If you miss the layup, you have to run two more. Its main purpose and value was to help the players pass on the run and build camaraderie, that sense of working together to achieve something and to see what happens when one player makes a mistake. But it was also a pretty good running drill, a good finisher for a hard practice when the guys might have a tendency to let up on their concentration, something you want to avoid.

In the NCAAs

We've been to the NCAAs eleven times during my career as a coach and we've always given a good account of ourselves because I never made a federal case out of it. The tournament is like icing on the cake to us. You go there knowing you've had a good year and that's why you get to go. As you prepare for it, you treat it like any other game—it's hard to do but you say, "All right, we're playing one more game. If we win that, then we'll play the next game." We took the psychology out of it, the idea that every team was superior, that everyone was so much better. We just played the game: how we felt we could beat the other team, what their weaknesses were, what we had to do, and if we held on to our guts, this is what would happen and for the most part it did.

That's how we prepared for UCLA last year. I told the team then the same thing I told my team when we played UCLA in the regular season in 1969 and lost by a point, 76–75, at the buzzer: "Don't go for offensive rebounds, because we're not going to get them anyway. Every time UCLA gets the ball and comes downcourt they have to see a cluster of five players with no holes protecting our basket." We did that for most of both games. Their '69 team was averaging 106 points a game and all five of their players went into the NBA, led by Sidney Wicks and Henry Bibby. We led that game the entire way until the end, when Wicks hit a jump shot from the side.

In last year's game, we got a total of six offensive rebounds. What's interesting is that UCLA only got six, too, which would suggest that they couldn't penetrate our defense once we slowed their fast break. We thought we could take advantage of their close guarding with some back-doors, and that's the play that we used to score the winning basket. Our center Steve Goodrich faked a pass to Gabe Lewullis who seemed to be cutting away from the basket. His defender went for the fake. Lewullis reversed direction, ran for the hole, took a perfect bounce pass from Goodrich and scored on a layup. Maybe if we play UCLA 100 times, they would win 99, but we got the one that counted.

Our Georgetown NCAA game in 1989 presented an interesting challenge. We had won the league and were sitting around on Sunday waiting for the announcement of the pairings. The Big East had just finished its tournament and Georgetown ran roughshod over everybody. I'm sitting at home waiting and the players are over at someone's room eating pizza, watching television, and waiting, and they announce we're playing Georgetown. All of a sudden that pizza didn't taste so good. We had a week to prepare, and for the first three days the team was scared. Then I told them about the '69 game against UCLA. I told them we hadn't had any time to prepare and how we stayed in there. We expected a press and we tried to get ready for it by playing against a press in practice that turned out to be even more vicious than Georgetown's. Everyone else had tried to dribble against Georgetown's press, but we threw over it. Well, we managed to stay in the game early against Georgetown, and with every minute, as you realize you can play a team like that, your confidence grows and you see you're going to be okay. Our center, Kit Mueller, could not be rattled and was tough. We had this little point guard, George Leftwich, who played the whole game with one turnover, and Bobby Scrabis was our best shooter. It was an excellent team. The longer we stayed in the game, the more pressure that put on Georgetown. We went ahead by as many as eight points, only to lose on a pretty controversial shot by Scrabis with time running out—whether it was blocked clean or he was fouled . . . we lost by one point, 50–49. We had three days of euphoria after that because we had given them such a good game, then we got sick as hell as it dawned on us we could have won: If we had gotten a couple of more rebounds, or the referee had called the foul on the last shot by Scrabis, or if we had not taken a shot when we did, or whatever. It was the kind of game where you have to

156

play a perfect game to win, or if you make a mistake you have to be lucky and get away with it. But I wouldn't call it a good loss. There are no good losses.

A Coach's Heart

When I lose, I take my losses hard. It's my prerogative. But when my team works hard, no matter what the score, I am with them.

Home Court

Playing on your home court can mean a lot. Away, the size of the court is the same, but the background is different and the intensity of the crowd can be a factor. The fact that the home team practices there every day—shoots at the same baskets every day—and gets used to the background is an advantage. They know the bounce of the floor, the lighting. They're used to their own crowd, its level of noise and excitement. And referees are influenced by the noise of the crowd. Out at Las Vegas in 1990, the crowd noise drowned out the game; the players could not hear us call timeout. The last year before Rutgers moved into its new gym, we played over there and there was so much noise when Rutgers went ahead that I called timeout, and the building was shaking, actually shaking —the floor and the walls. When my guys came off the floor they were so damn scared, but that team had a lot of guts and came back and actually went ahead before we blew it at the end because we couldn't handle their press. We played up at Seton Hall once when their furnace had broken and their players were complaining about the cold. Our gym at Princeton, Jadwin, is always cold, so we were used to it and beat them by 25 points. The Palestra is always a tough place to play; so are Brown and Cornell. There's always a feeling of electricity in the atmosphere at the Palestra and the place is always full, the fans close at hand.

When you're on the road, you try to offset the advantage by not thinking about it. When the roar of the crowd gets really difficult, I tell my guys, "That's when you turn on the juice, work harder, concentrate more." I like to have my team shoot around before a game in an opponent's gym to get familiar with the surroundings—that's pretty standard—but it doesn't neutralize the home court advantage. Your attitude, your ability to concentrate on working hard and doing the right things, the things you do every day, are what help you overcome the other team's home court advantage.

Stay off Your Legs?

I don't tell my guys to stay off their legs the day before a game. When you mention to your guys the possibility of their getting tired, you're instilling an idea they've probably never thought about. I worry about guys who think about getting tired.

■ ■ ■

Team Camaraderie

How do you know your team has camaraderie? I can tell by the way they walk off the floor at the end of a practice. You can feel their happiness vibrating; you can see how they work out together; you can watch it in the shower room—what they're talking about, the level of excitement. There are so many ways you can feel it, and it's better to feel it than to hear it. "Heard melodies are sweet, but those unheard are sweeter," John Keats said. The camaraderie practically comes out of their bodies. After they're done playing, they become friends for life—that's one of the most significant and enduring features of a team sport. And you don't feel that way when you're losing. When you lose you hear a lot of bitching and moaning. Losing reveals things.

A Bad Win

A bad win is one where you score more points but they've outplayed, outsmarted, and outworked you. But things happened and you were successful, though you know when you walk off that you were outplayed. That's a bad win—there might be another word or two that describes better what happened, but someone called it a bad win. It could be a lucky win, or an undeserved win. Regardless, the point is that whatever you call it, a bad win is still better than a good loss.

■　■　■

Nothing Else but Luck

A guy makes a fifty-foot shot at the buzzer to win a game —that is luck. The shot that almost won the Georgetown game for us—was it blocked or was it a foul? Whichever, it was bad luck. A shot off the back of the rim pops straight up in the air fifteen feet and falls back through—that is luck. The harder you work, the luckier you get. You make your own luck—I support every one of those clichés, but there are some occasions when there's nothing you can say except that they were lucky.

I remember once we were playing Cornell and were down to the last shot, trailing by one point. We designed a play for our best shooter, and somehow the ball ended up in the hands of our worst shooter, who threw up a bank shot and scored for the win. It had nothing to do with anything we had planned and it certainly had nothing to do with Cornell's hard work through the game—but they lost.

My 1987–88 team was one of the unluckiest teams I've ever seen. We lost to La Salle on a fifty-foot shot, and if that wasn't bad enough, the ball hit the front of the rim and popped up in the air eight feet so that you had to wait for it to go up and come down to see yourself lose. Then we lost to Brown on another fifty-footer. We lost to Cornell when Dave Orlandini stole the ball at half-court and drove downcourt for an uncontested layup, and the referee blows the whistle when he gets to the foul lane and says he committed a foul on the steal. We lost 60–55. Then when Cornell came to Princeton at the end of the season, we killed them, 79–58; Cornell had won the league by then but my guys knew they were better. It was hard for them to leave the locker room.

Luck works the other way, too. We beat Oklahoma State by

three points in the 1983 NCAA tournament. They had trouble with our zone defense, made a lot of turnovers, had a hard time scoring. We defended against their inside game, but they had just won the Big Eight Tournament and, like lots of teams, they regarded us lightly as an Ivy League team—there's always a complacency factor when a team plays an Ivy team. As we got down to the end, one of my guys made a mistake on his slide in the zone and Oklahoma had an easy, wide-open shot but they didn't see it and we got away with it. If you make a mistake in a close game, you need to get away with it. That's another case of luck.

Rough on Refs

I was tough to referee a game for. I want the referees to be totally fair. I don't want them to influence the game in the least. You have to remember that with our players, we have to do so many little things to be successful; if we're off by just this much—because of a bad or lazy ref—many of our close wins turn into close losses.

I've been thrown out of two games in my career, against Virginia and against Massachusetts. There are times when you'd like to say something but you know it's futile. You look out there and what you see is City Hall and you cannot beat City Hall. I've seen about half a dozen good refs. We lost to Connecticut one year up there, lost by 10, and I thought the crew of refs was really good. After the game I went up to them, and I guess they expected I was going to give them a ton of crap, but I said, "Fellows, thanks for giving us a chance to win." They were taken aback.

But there are some referees who are dishonest. They try to determine the outcome of the game in favor of one particular team, because they referee on that court too many times. Not too many of them are dishonest, but you do run into them, always on the road, and they have a lot to do with what happens. One time we were playing a top-ranked team on their court. It was a close game—we're leading—and we start the second half. Suddenly, my team has seven fouls to their one, and they're the ones who are pressing. Now you explain that.

Being a referee is no different from being a player: He has the same set of responsibilities, which means he has to be in shape, know the rules, be fearless, call what he sees, and not try to please players or coaches. You want the referee to put his whole heart into the game, to do as good a job as he can do. But sometimes he referees your game the night after a big game for which he received a higher fee, say he got $900 on a Thursday night; when he gets $250 for your game on the next night he might just give you a $250 job.

Care How You Play

Certain life parts of the game affect the way you play. There are a growing number of players and coaches who don't adhere to that. When you cross the court line, they think nothing else matters; I don't subscribe to that: I think a certain amount of caring is involved and affects how you play.

We had a player here named Paul Friedman ('81) who did everything he could to be a good player. His sophomore year, he developed cancer, but he continued to help coach jayvees. Here was this guy fighting an illness that proved terminal,

162

continuing his studies, and helping to coach the jayvees—
that's the highest level of courage, of love and caring for what
you are trying to do that I have ever seen.

Fame

An athlete's fame dies young. It's the same with a
coach. Somebody is going to replace you as a coach and make
more or less of a contribution. A college coach has the life
expectancy of a second lieutenant in combat.

Somewhere along the line, some players get the idea that
fame is a tremendous thing. The drive for recognition today is
strong, very strong. But it's so unnecessary. You ought to do
things for the right reasons: the satisfaction of doing something well with real integrity; the pleasure after a hard-fought
game, especially when you're the victor; the camaraderie of
being with your teammates in the locker room talking about
the game and how much fun it was, and what hard work. If
you do, you get a satisfaction that public acclaim can never
give you. Fame comes out second, by far; in the long run you
forget all the notoriety, but not your teammates.

At my retirement picnic, the kind I used to have every year
after school, about seventy players came back with their families to see their old coach. Though I was happy about seeing
them, what was exhilarating was that they treated each other
like they'd never been away from each other. They just picked
up right where they left off as teammates. It was a great day.

■ ■ ■

Learn Any Offense in Thirty Minutes

It wouldn't take me one half hour to learn the offensive system of any coach. We can then prepare for that team's offense by rehearsing their system until we know it as well as they do. It's harder to prepare for a team that is highly skilled in the basics of the game and can do anything because they're so highly skilled.

What Can Youngsters Learn?

Some kids come to my basketball camp because their parents want to get rid of them for a week. Others come just for social reasons, and in some cases that's a good enough reason. If they learn nothing else, they learn how to get along with other kids—you learn cooperation. That's one of the chief values of sports. But camp kids who sit around the juke box or hang out in the camp store are never going to be good players.

Sometimes, parents send their kids to my camp and expect me to teach them all about basketball in one week. In one week—it's unbelievable! It cannot be done. I had a kid show up in my camp one year with a flashy uniform. His mother told me she had spent $100 to buy it. I watched him, and the way he played, he would have been better off in rags.

What we can teach youngsters in one week is how to work, because if they learn how to work hard, then they can use those work habits both in basketball and in all aspects of life.

In camp they can also learn about competition. You have to do better than the guy next to you who might be your friend.

How do you go about doing that? You compete, and competition brings out both the good and bad. I see a kid age ten who trips somebody going in for a layup, or starts to cry when you criticize him, or cheats on the score, or is selfish, or doesn't pay attention to the coach, or doesn't understand why you do drills. Maybe I can help him learn how to begin to modify his behavior.

Take a young kid who cries when he loses. You can't be happy about losing, but you don't have to go kill yourself either, because there's always a next time—though you want to try not to let it happen too often.

Out of every group of seventeen or eighteen kids who come to camp, some kid will return to camp the next year because he has both the interest and the skill level. As his skills improve, he'll advance to harder camps where the nature of the competition is more intense, and where he has to rise to that level if he's going to survive. He'll keep going until he reaches the uppermost level of his ability, the maximum height of his development curve. Somewhere along the line, some coach or maybe more than one coach will have an impact on this kid. And if he's lucky, it will be a positive impact—some thought, some idea of behavior that will stay with him a long time, if not the rest of his life.

One thing I notice about young kids: They are so eager to learn and they generally have fantastic work habits—they want to play all day and night if you let them. Teaching them can also be one of the hardest things in the world to do. You spend half the time just getting them quiet and disciplining them. At the end of a school year, the average teacher needs a rest. Having to discipline students or players interferes with what you're trying to do; sometimes the teacher or coach burns out and stops watching his students, stops demanding

165

that they do their best. You try not to let it happen, but you don't always succeed.

A Good High School Coach

A good high school coach is the salt of the earth. And when his teams are well coached, a college coach is the direct beneficiary of all his work. When players who have had good high school coaching walk on the floor in college, there isn't much that coach has to do. I've had fifteen to twenty kids like that where the coaching was so good I did not have to do a thing. I cannot emphasize enough what it means to start with that great coach at the sixth or seventh grade who tries to get kids to do things better. Grade school coaches are the unsung heroes of this country and they're disappearing because it takes a lot of work and constant attention. Sometimes it is too much of a sacrifice.

Coaching High School Versus College

One difference between high school and college coaching is that you have to develop more understanding of the players' different interests in college. I'm not saying you have to accept or give into those other interests—you just have to understand them, and you have to help them understand the difference between understanding and compromising.

Another difference is that you spend a lot of time in college looking for good players. In high school, you spend a lot of time trying to make players good.

The Rat Race

Recruiting is harder now than it was twenty years ago. No player in this country goes unnoticed, which makes competition for the players much greater. There might be more players, but I don't know if there is as much talent as there used to be.

The whole recruiting scene is out of whack: Athletes are not going to college for the right reasons. They get so much exposure, so much publicity that they come to college with inflated egos. We had a kid who came to Princeton on an unofficial visit as a junior. He was great, liked the school and all that. That fall, some big-time schools chased him. He came to visit us after that and wanted to know if we traveled first-class. We couldn't stand him anymore, and he went somewhere else.

If you want to get into the rat race, you've got to be a rat. I found that the more you had to kiss a player's rear end to go to your school, the more you had to kiss his rear end to play. I had the most luck with players who wanted to be there from the beginning.

Recruiting alters the player-coach relationship. I always wanted to teach; I never wanted to be a salesman. That's the job of an encyclopedia salesman, or the guy pushing vacuum cleaners. It has the potential for tarnishing a wholesome relationship between player and coach. That may be the reason Bob Cousy quit coaching. One coach was telling me recently that kids are getting rougher today. It's not like it used to be, of course—nothing is. But their behavior: players punching out their girlfriends, stealing cars, breaking bottles over people's heads. Coaches complain, but they're partly responsible because the recruiting process is such you gotta compromise your principles to get a player. And that destroys the coach-player relationship.

My first year at Princeton, I think I behaved badly. I had guys eating at my house. Finally, I said, "Holy Christ, this is not for me. No way I am going to get on my knees to talk to kids." We were probably the lowest-key, maybe the worst recruiters in the Ivies, because I don't like it, and because we were too honest. We'd tell a kid if he could or couldn't play for us. He might come to Princeton anyway and not play, but I wanted him to feel that while I might be wrong about him, I didn't lie to him. I told a prospect to work on his weaknesses, what he should do to get better. Sometimes they took that very well, other times not.

Next, I'd tell a prospect that this was the hard way. There is no compromise at Princeton in terms of what you have to do. You struggle with a tough paper in history class and get a feeling of elation when you finally complete it, then as you head to practice you realize you have another paper due in three days—and this goes on for four years. And, of course, I'd tell the parents they must be disposed to make a financial commitment, since there are no athletic scholarships in the Ivy League. The basic problem is that the more recruited and pampered an athlete is, the more untruths he is told, the more he expects, and I had to try to get him to commit to something that is hard when he could go somewhere else for free and have an easy time.

168

Burglars Get into Homes, Too

In college, the more successful you are the more apt you are to become a whore. I once met a coach who told me he had been in fifty homes one winter to visit prospects. Fifty homes! He sounded like the president of the American Burglars Association. They get into homes, too. And whatever you have to do to induce a player to come you have to do the same things to get him to play. Thirty years ago, the coaches used to be tyrants. Now, it's the players.

Three-Car-Garage Guys

The shrewd coach rarely recruits players from schools whose names include the words "country," "day," or "friends," and don't forget "école." Players who are products of the kind of affluence those names suggest are never tough enough when the game is on the line. You can't win with three-car-garage guys. With two-car-garage guys you got a chance. I was a no-car-garage guy in a $21-a-month apartment by Quinn's coal yard in Bethlehem.

I liked to find players from schools whose names begin with "bishop" or "monsignor"—city Catholic schools—because they have learned discipline and because they tend to be shrewd, tough, hardworking, loyal to their friends and families.

■ ■ ■

Can He Pass?

The first thing I look for in a high school player is, Can he pass? If he can, he's the same guy who can cut, and can defend. He's the guy who sees everything, the man he is passing to, the players around him, the opportunities for creativity. That is a gift of DNA, God, whatever. It can't be taught. Armond Hill was a tremendous passer and dribbler who saw everybody on the court and could run a team, as he did the Hawks when he got to the NBA. He had a great sense of team and how to play without smothering his teammates. He also had long arms and the right size. I don't think he worked hard enough at shooting; he would shoot for half an hour, and then you would look at the other end of the court and he would be down there feeding passes to some kids. Armond came to visit us at our camp one year and told us he was working hard on his shooting. We found him in the gym with five young kids who were shooting and he was feeding them. He wasn't selfish enough about improving his own skills.

Character Shows

I don't recruit players who are nasty to their parents. That shows me they are giving less than they can give and can't forge the bonds essential for a good team.

I look for players who understand that the world does not revolve around them.

I remember watching a kid once in a pickup game who knew I was there, and he fired up a bunch of shots, making only a few. After the game, he apologized to me for his poor marksmanship and said he had trouble getting used to the other players. I told him that when he learned to shoot less, he would get used to the other guys.

Lightbulbs

There are certain players I call lightbulbs. They possess the essence of life as basketball players. When they come on the court, they light up the gym. I cannot name five players at Princeton who were lightbulbs, but I can name fifty.

Look Beyond Talent

My ideal player loves to play, constantly learns, has good character, does not give in to defeat. He uses all the parts of his abilities, not just one particular thing. I want a kid who goes ahead and does what he knows has to be done, who doesn't give himself an excuse to fail.

My best recruiting experience was when I went to see Frank Sowinski ('77), who became one of our top players, but not a household name elsewhere. He played in a suburban league, and I wasn't sure he could play for us. I had seen him play before, and this time, he didn't play that well. He got three fouls early on and fouled out. His mother said after the game, "Guess you don't want him now." I said, "I want him more than ever." I saw how he behaved. He didn't sulk or pout—he cheered for his team. When he got to Princeton, he became a great player. Another time, a guy I was watching came out of the game and gave his coach a bunch of tongue. I left the game. You've got to have talent—you can't get to first base otherwise—but I look for other things, too.

The Campus Tour

When a prospect visited campus, I'd take him to the gym first and talk about the national caliber of our schedule and tell him how hard things were going to be at Princeton. I'd take him to the library, to the chapel, and once in a while to a dormitory and a classroom. I'd tell him the library is the heart of the university and that he's going to have to spend a lot of time there. No university can be anything without a great library. I remember one recruit who read an essay that one of my players was writing for a history course and immediately decided not to pursue his application here.

When Mickey Steurer first visited campus, he was a senior from Archbishop Molloy in New York and had averaged 17 points a game as a guard. I'd seen him play and liked what I saw: the way he passed the ball, the controlled shots, his court sense. He seemed aware of everything that was happening and he was poised; no matter what happened, his expression never changed. His father was a policeman whose precinct included Bedford-Stuyvesant during the riots of the 1960s, times that he said were harder than World War II when he parachuted from a burning airplane into Romania and spent seven months in a prison camp. Frank McGuire at South Carolina had offered Mickey a full ride, but Mickey wasn't sure the coach really wanted him. Still, he visited there and

North Carolina, St. Bonaventure, and Holy Cross along with Princeton. When he visited those places he had a great time. When he came to Princeton, one of my players met him at the bus stop on his bicycle and they went back to his room for a pizza. He slept on a mattress in the dorm. It was also the week of the NBA championships and the Knicks were playing. Back home, everyone was tuned into their televisions, but at Princeton the TV sets were turned off because it was midterm week and everyone was studying. I told him that I could not guarantee him anything. I had another guard coming, Armond Hill, and I was pretty sure he would start for three years. I needed a mate for Hill. I told him he needed to practice his dribbling, especially going to his left. I don't think he liked that. I found out later that he thought it was all pretty weird. With my bow tie and cigar, he thought I looked like the guy who worked in a Buster Brown shoe store that he'd been going to since he was six. But his father liked me because I wasn't slick or pushy. And Mickey had seen us play on television and thought he could play here. And in the end, when he got admitted, his father told him that no matter what happened in basketball, nobody could ever take Princeton away from him. He respected his dad's opinion and he came, telling himself that he was going to prove that he could play. And he did.

Don't Worry About Tuition

There were some coaches who used to tell prospects not to worry about Princeton's high tuition, because when they graduated the Princeton name would help them find

173

good jobs as bankers, lawyers, and stockbrokers and they would get their investment back quickly. I never did. I talked to them in terms of destiny: I'd tell them they were going to have to take care of their own destiny at Princeton, by themselves, though I'd also tell them that the Princeton name might make it easier for them to take care of that destiny.

The biggest thing Princeton does, and what the kids need to understand, is that the university makes it impossible for them not to learn how to do things for themselves. At other places, so many people are dependent on each other; they wait for others to help. Everyone who walks out of Princeton knows they can do things well. The job of the university is not to make any student happy; that's the student's job. The university's job is to create a framework for learning, thinking, and studying. A university is bigger than all of us and some prospects don't understand that.

Admissions

When God created me, He also made the Princeton Admission Office. That is a parody of a poem by Thomas Hardy, "Convergence of the Twain," about the entwined fates of the *Titanic* and the iceberg. Sometimes I would see a kid I would love to have and who would love to come. He is smart and capable of doing the work, but I know they are going to shoot him down at the Admission Office.

They're an obstacle, but they're not the only one. The parent of a kid I was pursuing one year—who had been admitted —called me after getting the admission letter and said, "Coach Carril, you're terrific. I want my son to play for you.

But you are not worth the $20,000 tuition fee I would have to pay to send him." I lived with that for twenty-nine years and each year it got tougher and tougher.

Yes for the Shot Clock

The shot clock was instituted to stop people from holding the ball. Though some people think that Princeton, with its cerebral, methodical, admittedly slow-paced offensive strategy, would have had something to do with the origin of the shot clock, I think more than anything it was those teams that used the four-corner offensive strategy first developed by Dean Smith at the University of North Carolina. That tactic resulted in some games with scores of 10–8 and 12–10. They usually occurred in tournaments, when a low seed decided its only chance at winning was to hold the ball and force a low score. The shot clock was established to combat that.

We never had a score like that. If you were to ask which school or program would be most affected by a shot clock, half the people would pick Princeton. In fact, I voted for the 45-second clock, the original time for the shot clock. That always comes as a complete surprise to everybody. I did it, I have to admit, for selfish reasons: Before it was instituted, we were playing a zone defense, which nobody seemed able to attack. If you look at our films of that era, you'd discover that our opponents were holding the ball against us because they thought they couldn't beat our zone defense. You'd also discover that there wasn't that much difference between the average span of time between shots for us and our opponents. Against UCLA last year in the first round of the NCAA, we averaged a shot every twenty-five seconds, while during one stretch UCLA shot every twenty-four seconds. I wanted the other team to shoot faster, and I knew a shot clock would force the other team to speed up. But, because of our deliberate offense, the perception persisted that we were holding the ball, slowing down the game. When the 45-second clock didn't do enough to quicken the pace, the limit dropped to thirty-five seconds.

At thirty-five seconds, I began to see some decline in the cerebral nature of the game—the gap between talent and no talent is widened by the 35-second clock. It became harder for a team of less talent to pull an upset.

I would be against going lower, to a 24-second clock, like the pros. There are some up-tempo devotees who want to speed the game up even more to please the crowd. I think they're confused about what constitutes real entertainment value in basketball. They don't understand that entertainment is at its highest level when the competition is at its highest level. Look at some of those NBA playoff games—that's competition, and that's entertainment. Princeton always enjoys high ratings on ESPN—in fact, among the highest. Our games have been close, competitive, and entertaining—because there was some kind of design to the game strategy and execution, and even the average fan could see what we were doing to give us a chance to win. With a 24-second clock, I don't think you would have enough time to execute your strategy. Teams like us need time to probe and pick at the defense, to execute plays that exploit the other team's defense and help even out the contest. The 24-second clock makes the shooter more important in the NBA than in college and would make the game more of a run-and-gun affair, which would wipe out the cerebral nature of college basketball.

Our Toughest Opponents

The teams that have had trouble beating us are teams that tried to outsmart us. The teams that caused us the most trouble have always been those who play helter-skelter and succeed in changing our way of playing. We would have won a hundred fewer games if the opposing coach had told his players, "Look, throw the ball up to the basket. I don't care if it goes in or not, just go get it." Instead, they tried to outsmart us by playing exactly the way we did. It made it harder for us, but it kept us in the game.

You Against Yourself

Princeton is a tough school. Basketball is a relief from studies. If you're in an environment where all you have to do is fool around and you can still make it, that's what you'll do. If you're in another environment where you can't fool around and have to put your nose to the grindstone and study, that's what you'll do instead. Players would ask me how they can compete with the quality of student here. I tell them they don't; you compete with yourself. It's what you do versus what you could do that counts. Life or basketball, it's all the same.

Heart

If you have a good strong heart, you can overcome your environment, whatever it is.

The Coach's Role

When you prepare to play a game, you first look over the talent of your opponent to see how you're going to beat them. Against Notre Dame in 1977, when we won 76–62, we anticipated a press but felt they didn't protect their backcourt well enough, so we beat their press with long passes that produced seven or eight uncontested layups. Against North Carolina in 1971, ranked number three when we played them, we thought they would overplay us and that we could run our back-door. We did, thirty to forty times, maybe more, and beat them 89–73. And with UCLA last year, we decided not to go for offensive rebounds. Once a game starts, the coach has to see whether what you're doing works, and be ready to make a change. In general, when you're overmatched you have to make the game shorter, and the way you do that is by making the points longer, by not shooting as quickly. After about eight minutes on the average, a coach should have a pretty good idea of what's going on.

Once the game starts, you can do a little bit of changing at halftime. But most of what the team does is what the coach prepared in practice; that's where you teach your players the general philosophy of how to play that game. Against Wisconsin a few years ago, we were down by 14 points at halftime, and all I did in the locker room was yell. Our play was so disgraceful. Wisconsin scored the first basket of the second half to go up by 16 points, and then we went on to win by five. After the game, a professor came up to me and said, "I teach, and I would like to know what you told your guys at halftime." I looked at him and said, "I don't think you would." My guys were a disgrace to themselves. Sometimes there are things to tell them, and sometimes there is very little to tell.

178

Whatever you tell them, it must relate to the manner in which they played.

Playing to win, you have to subjugate your own personal desires to the role that's required of you to win. Some guys don't like that. Remember, some guys walk out of a losing game having scored 25 points and are perfectly content. If you have guys like that on your team, you're not going to win too many games. You cannot ever forget the human equation in sports.

I think I'm a good preparation coach. St. John's is hard to beat anywhere, anytime, but we beat them in the 1975–76 season, 58–55, because we noticed in scouting them that their center never came out to defend screens. We had our center dribble over to anyone who could shoot; our guy would come off the dribble screen and the center never came out. That was our whole game plan, and it worked so well they finally had to take the center out of the game. Another time, against South Carolina in 1992, we thought we could get a back-door off an out-of-bounds play. We waited for the right situation, and then when we were up by one we ran it and scored to go up by three and eventually win.

The biggest challenge for me over the years has been to keep my head during a game. I am not the best at that. You have to keep your head so that you can watch what's going on. I pride myself on being able to tell my players that there is not one single thing we practice that is not going to show up in a game, and anything new that does show up is my responsibility. Jack Rohan at Columbia and Dave Gavitt at Dartmouth used to cause me some difficulty; they played a combination defense, and I had trouble figuring out what they were doing. I didn't have the right antidote to their defenses.

During a game, I ask my players what's going on. I'd ask

Sowinski or Armond or Kit Mueller, how do we want to play this out-of-bounds play. Or, I'd say, "Let's do this," and look at Kit and he'd shake his head and I'd say, "Okay, let's get another play." Joe Scott ('87) would say, "Coach, let's do this . . ." and so on. As a matter of fact, I think I should have done a little more of this because you can't see everything that is going on. Chuck Daly, who used to coach at Penn, says that when he went into the NBA to coach, he learned a lot from just watching what each player would do. I expect to do that, too. Having good assistant coaches is important, too, and I'd ask them for help. Most of the time I have a feel for what's going on myself, but good assistants are a big help.

Playing Catch-Up

Over the years, people have faulted me for our deliberate style of play, saying that it's hard for us to catch a team that has opened up a lead. They say we don't score fast enough to close any gap. I don't agree with that. We've had many games here where we were down by as much as 20 and managed to get back and tie or win. Against Arkansas, we were down by 16 points, and with a minute to go we were up by one. We pecked away at it. By trying to be even more deliberate, by not panicking, by not trying to play a style of offense that you aren't good at and haven't practiced you can catch up. Play your game, get two here, three there, one here, and pretty soon the score adds up.

On the other hand, if you're down by eight and decide to press even though you aren't great at it, you can end up down by 20 quickly. It's like a boxer who can't punch, and instead of using cunning and opportunity he flails away, and loses.

Whichever way a team chooses to catch up has to reflect its normal style of play. We have been down by 16, 18, 20 points a lot of times and come back because we understood what to do. You have to know what you're good at doing and do it.

Use Your Assets

If my Princeton teams had superior speed, we would have played the fast-break-and-shoot style, the whole court, but since we didn't we advanced the ball more methodically, half a court at a time. And while we played hard defense, our slower style of offense made it easier for us to maintain our pace for the entire game. We passed, we cut, we shot the ball well and we looked for good shots. The main thing was to get a good shot every time down the floor. We were patient and disciplined. If that's old-fashioned, then I am guilty. You have to take advantage of what you have. Marilyn Monroe and Sophia Loren did that, and we do it, too. If you have a fast team and you don't run, you're being stupid. And if you have a slow team, you must take the run out of the game.

Sixth Man

Sometimes you hear coaches and fans say that a certain player performs better as a substitute than as a starter. I do not believe in that stuff. If you can play, you can play. The rest shouldn't matter. However, if you feel a player is more comfortable by being a sixth man, then do it.

Blowout Against North Carolina

We got clobbered in a game against North Carolina in the 1968–69 season (103–76), and afterward I told my team that I thought we had disgraced ourselves. It was a consolation game in a tournament and we went in with a "consolatory" attitude. When things started going downhill, we died. We hustled and scrapped to stay in the thing, then they pulled ahead by ten points, or whatever it was, and we stopped. I was quoted in the papers as saying we had disgraced ourselves, and I took some criticism for that. Somebody asked me, "What are the players going to think when they read in the paper that you said they were a disgrace?" I said I didn't care what they thought. What I was saying was the truth. They were not kids; they were adults. People their age were dying in Vietnam. These guys were lucky to be playing basketball. It's okay to go under in a basketball game, but if you do, do it only after you've tried everything else.

Avoid the Ups and Downs

We had a game against Rutgers at Jadwin that they won. After the game, they went crazy and carried on. They would not leave the gym. I tell my guys that when we win, we should feel proud we were victors, to realize what we did, but that doesn't mean you go crazy and taunt the other team. It's the same when we lose: Examine what you did, and start to assess what you have to do to improve. You can have no glee about losing, but whether you win or lose on Thursday, either way, it cannot affect what you do on Friday. That's important to remember, and if you can learn that, you can learn to avoid ups and downs.

Mop-up Time

Sometimes in the last minute or two of a game, when you have players that you want to put in for mop-up time, you'll get one that doesn't want to go, like it's beneath him. When I was in high school, maybe tenth grade, I sat on the bench. And when it came to the end of a game, the coach would look down the bench. I would stick my head out as far as I could, so he would see me. Because even if I got in for just a minute, or a minute and a half, if I could do something good, the next time I would play more.

Character Witness

I was once asked by one of my players to be a character witness when he was called before the University's Discipline Committee. He had been caught shooting a BB gun at people. I could not believe it. I told the committee that he was a hard worker and I respected his work habits, but what he had done was wrong. He hasn't spoken to me since.

Are You Worthy?

Every now and then, we go through periods in this country where everyone wants to wear their patriotism on their sleeve—literally. That happened recently during the Persian Gulf War, when there was talk about putting flags on our basketball uniforms. This is what I thought about that, and what I said at the time:

What good is it if you wear a flag and play like a dog? What good is it if you put a yellow ribbon on your porch, or a flag on your lawn, and cheat on your taxes? That young soldier who was killed today defending our country—he can never be replaced. All the dreams and aspirations his family had for him, they are gone. How can there be any way to balance that except for every person in this country to do the best he can to honor that hero? Maybe it's far-fetched to think that someone on the front line is concerned whether our players go to class, but I think that is part of what they are fighting for. That if our students do not do everything in their power to keep their commitments to their parents, they are letting the whole country down. This kid who died over there today, you don't honor him just by putting something on your clothes; instead ask yourself, What are you doing in your life to make sure you are worthy of him?

■ ■ ■

Jetting In, Jetting Out

My high school coach inspired me to become a coach. When I was growing up, the country was getting out of the Depression, and WWII was going on—it was a different environment. Players now have so much more in life than I had, yet their lives are more complicated, harder, because the number of choices has expanded close to chaos. Today there are a lot of reasons why you might not have to do something. In my times, there were fewer reasons, fewer acceptable excuses. The pace is too fast now. Does anybody have time for cracker-barrel philosophizing? At coaching clinics, the big-time coaches don't hang around any more. They jet in, give their talks, and jet out.

NBA Draft

It is not good for kids, or for the NBA to draft players out of high school. And I object to the hypocrisy of college coaches saying the kids are going to miss their college education when, in fact, as things stand now at many of the big basketball schools, they don't really get that much of a college education.

They Don't Show Up, but You See Them

There are so many things that don't show up on the stat sheet, or in the win and loss column, that no one can explain, but you see them and they affect the outcome of games. There are hundreds of them: Players who learn how to do something just by watching compared to those who watch the same demonstration and can't do it; who go after loose balls and come up with every one of them as opposed to someone who tries just as hard and comes up with none; or the player who can smell out every rebound and get it while another player who jumps a foot over the rim doesn't get a single one. How is it that one guy can deflect a pass over and over again and another cannot? And when you see him do it, you want to teach all your guys that and you start saying, "Use your hands!" and some of them get a little better at it, and some who work just as hard never do. Occasionally, we come down on a two-on-one situation, and I yell to the defender, "Play the pass." He lunges at the man with the ball knowing he is going to throw it to his teammate, and steals the pass, and seems able to do that repeatedly. And then there's the player you know is going to get a bad cold midway through the season and he does. And the other player who never gets hurt or sick. Why?

Many times I ask myself the question, "Am I trying to teach this player instinct, or am I teaching him a skill?" Whether you're trying to teach a college player or a seven-year-old, you are looking for instinct. There are ten programs in this country that get the majority of the top fifty players each year, and they're looking for the same intangibles. We had some ten-year-old kids at our camp this year who were already competitors, while another bunch of ten-year-olds don't even know what that means. Why is that?

You ask that question a lot when you're coaching. A coach at a small school, he looks at a less-talented player to see if he can divine whether the guy is going to be good or even great. You're always recruiting someone who you hope is going to get better than he is, and you don't know why he isn't better at that moment, and you just hope the ability to get better is inside him and just hasn't been brought out yet. You don't know before you recruit a player who misses five straight shots whether he's the kind of kid who is going to take the sixth shot. Those are the intangibles. They can't be explained, but you see the results and you're always looking for them.

Year-End Review

Every year, I look at the films of the last season and try to see whether our breakdowns are because of poor teaching or sloppy execution. I want to know if I'm insisting on teaching something we just cannot do well, and I want to figure out a few things we do well and concentrate on those for the new season. If you had a good season and you're happy, you may feel you don't want to look at the films too much, and if you had a bad season and you're down, you don't want to look at them even more because they depress you.

Sometimes when you lose a guy, it changes everything you're going to do. The year after we lost to Georgetown in the NCAA's, we had the entire team back except for Bobby Scrabis, who was worth about 17 to 18 points a game for us. We needed those 18 points, so that year we had a kid who had transferred in a year earlier and sat out the season—Sean Jackson. He was a good shooter and was going to get us those points, which meant somebody had to sit and it ended up being someone who wasn't even playing Scrabis's position. It was the right decision, but it didn't make the guy sitting very happy.

Not Enough Creative Coaching

When I speak at clinics, I tell the coaches that I don't think there is enough creative thinking going on, not enough of them are thinking of new ideas, new ways to do things to help their teams. I remember once spending forty-five minutes speaking about defensive play and as soon as I finished, a coach raised his hand and asked me if I could show him a good inbounds play to use.

How I Get Along with Parents

I've had good relations with parents basically because I have been careful to be honest about the school and basketball and how these fit into the life of their son. If the parent only sees what his son is doing and not what the rest of the team is doing and how he relates to his teammates, it is almost always counterproductive.

I was at a high school game once watching a prospect. He was a shooter, and that night he scored his one thousandth point. They stopped the game and his mother and father and sister all came down from the stands. If he'd had a dog, it would have come, too. The parents either didn't see or didn't value all the people responsible for their son's being in position to score: the passer, the rebounder, the teammate setting the screen. If they see only the points and the glory instead of the whole team playing together to win, then their view is warped.

Parents have to ask themselves what effect they have on the players. You have parents at games, and afterward they come down and wait outside the locker room. Out come the players —their sons—some who played and some who didn't and might not ever. What effect does that have on the parents, and how does the way it affects them affect the players? It isn't easy to watch your son not play. Very few parents can cheer for a team when their son isn't playing. It takes a special kid, and a special parent. Remember, we have some parents who want their kid to be a star. When we lose a game but their son scores 27 points, the parents are totally elated. That is not easy for anyone, including—especially—me.

What is the role of the parent? I know parents who take their kids to the gym when they're young and just want them to shoot, or give their kids money for every basket they score in a game. They have tunnel vision. They ought to be supportive, to be interested, to want their sons to succeed, but not to interfere, and not to look for someone to blame if their son does not succeed. And they have to remember that when I tell them their son is great on Tuesday and criticize him on Thursday, I'm the same coach.

Religious Question

In January of 1970, we lost to UCLA 76–75 when Sidney Wicks hit a jump shot with three seconds to go. We

189

lost to Georgetown 50–49 in March 1989 in the last six seconds of the game. And to Penn, 51–50, in February 1990, on a tipped foul shot. I think when I am no longer in this world, I will have a nice talk with God. I will ask, "Why did You do this to me? Why pick me out for this? What did my grandfather do?" We had a few games like that. It made me question what's going on up there.

Competition Is Not Bad

One of the dominant themes in our society is competition. It is no accident that we shoot to win, or get high grades, or whatever. But when one or more competitors has to cheat, or do unwholesome things to win, or when the pressure, the greed gets so great they start to cheat, that doesn't mean competition is bad; it means they don't understand how to compete.

Competition is when equals go against each other. They give it the best they can, and afterward they shake hands. If the odds are all in one team's favor, then I don't think you can call it competition. When we beat Loyola Marymount in 1992, they had just lost the finals of their conference tournament, which dropped them from the NCAA tournament, and they had had to fly all the way across the country to play us. I thought it was unfair; the conditions were so much in our favor that I felt compelled to tell their coach that we would play them again on their court as soon as they had an opening. They came into a lion's den in Jadwin and we had every advantage. The edge, the competitive edge you're always looking for should come from your work habits, your preparation, your integrity, from everything you have to give; any other edge you're looking for, like a ref, a home court, a broken furnace in your gym—that's an abuse of the concept of competing.

Do What You Are Doing

The most important thing that you can do is to DO what you are doing well. The word "focus" does not carry the same weight with me, but another way of saying it is that the most important thing you can do on or off the court is to focus on what you are doing when you are doing it. That's key, that's key. I tell my players: "When you're out there on the court, basketball should be the most important thing. When you play, PLAY." A player finishes practice, showers, and goes back to his room to study: When you study, STUDY. Then it's not hard to separate the two. When you can concentrate on what you're doing it takes your mind off other things that might distract you. It leads to doing a lot of different things well.

Prideful

I have a lot of pride in what I do, but I never look and say I'm proud of myself. I don't even understand what that means. If there are things I have to do, I just do them.

College Sports Are Not Exempt

If you have a Congress unable to pass a budget, major stock market firms doing criminal things, an eight-billion-dollar drug problem, and we're giving helicopters to foreign countries for war—you cannot expect sports not to have problems. Sports are a reflection of our society.

Coaching My Way

I regularly got letters from irate fans of opposing teams telling me my style was bad for basketball. I remember Tom Young, when he coached at Rutgers, complaining to the press that he thought we held the ball too long—this was back before the shot clock. He advocated a thirty-second limit on holding the ball because, he said, the fans did not enjoy watching the ball be passed around more than thirty seconds. Well, I wasn't about to let the fans run my team, or Tom Young. If he had coached at Princeton, he would have coached the same way I did, and if I had coached up at Rutgers I would have coached the same way he did. The fans may or may not like a lot of passing, but I know they don't like losing. Results count no matter how you do it.

Coaching All-Stars

In July 1992, I coached a squad of all-stars at the Olympic Festival tryouts. Those players worried so much about how many minutes they were going to play, who was going to take the shot, who was going to do this or that. I finally told them, "You guys sleep together, you stay in the same dorm, you eat together—you do everything together except play together."

Spanish Pessimism

I guess one of the Spanish traits I inherited is pessimism. I always think things are worse than they are. I have a theory that all my good luck has run out, that I exhausted it when I was young because I had such fantastic teachers and coaches—I was so lucky to meet the right kind of people.

Anonymity at Princeton

I once took a friend on a sightseeing tour of the campus. When I drove in the main entrance, the uniformed guard at the gate challenged me because my car sticker had expired. He wasn't going to let me drive on the campus until someone passing by recognized me and could confirm that I worked for the university. I told my friend, "Do you think Dean Smith has to put up with this at Carolina? This is further evidence that around here you learn humility."

A few years ago, I was in a pizza parlor in town when a friend of mine came in with one of Princeton's deans. I was introduced and she held out her hand and said warmly, "And what, may I ask, do you do here?" "I coach basketball," I told her. My friend could not believe she didn't know who I was, and he asked me later if I was offended. "Nah," I told him. "I don't know what she does here, either."

"The Poor Guy"

Any coach of a small college who has aspirations of winning the national championship is unrealistic. For three weeks a year, during the tournament, you suffer. You think about the publicity, the acclaim. You think about the money and the television coverage. For three weeks a year, you might be tempted to take a pill or something. But, growing up, I was taught not to notice what others had and not to cry foul over the difference between what I have and what someone else might have. I've never worried about the difference.

When I finally go under, I am not going to have that national title. Who is going to walk by my grave and say, "Poor guy, never won a national title"? Nobody, right? That's not why you coach at a place like Princeton. You coach for the people who come through your program. You coach for guys who come and work as hard as you do. People told me I asked a lot from my kids, and I told them, Princeton kids have a lot to give. How much respect can you have for guys like that? You can't have enough.

■ ■ ■

Style Versus Substance

New Jersey Senator Bill Bradley has made some of the most important speeches I have ever heard about race relations, but his speeches don't seem to register with the audience. And then you get Ross Perot spouting out clichés that don't make any sense, and he gets 19 percent of the vote. What the hell is going on in this country?

I just got a new pair of Converse basketball shoes. They are practically all white, very simple design, comfortable sole—a terrific shoe, but the Converse guy tells me they aren't selling because they don't have enough fancy twirls and stuff on them. It's all style and no substance today. We pay athletes, give them cars and stereos, rationalize their bad behavior—people are defending the indefensible everywhere. What is going on in American sports? Our whole value system in the U.S. is under attack.

What I Value

My values, the things I have always tried to tell the players are: Make sure you do not count on anyone else but yourselves. Be prepared. Have a good work ethic. Be loyal to your friends. This is what is important.

■ ■ ■

What Kids Really Need

To me the most important thing a kid can have is two parents.

All I Ever Wanted

All I ever wanted as a coach was to get the best from every kid I had. And I have not improved one bit in that respect. I will never be able to understand why someone doesn't play his best all the time. I will never be able to understand that. A guy who gives you less than what he can give is, one, telling you what he thinks of you, and, two, telling you what he thinks of himself. And in both cases, it's bad. Now that's old-fashioned talk, but I don't think that is ever going to change for me, or for anybody.

No Middle Ground

I am not surprised I stayed at Princeton as long as I did. I could have had jobs at five to ten other places, but I stayed because at Princeton there doesn't seem to be a middle ground in terms of how things are done compared to most big-time places. I guess it would be possible to run a clean program at a big-time school. It's almost impossible not to at Princeton.

The Toughest Coach

Maybe I have been a tough coach, and maybe some of my players would like to punch me out, but it's been my observation that rather than hating me, over the long run the reverse happens, because it becomes clear that the things I taught them in basketball are the same things they encounter in their professions. They write me and tell me, "Coach, this is exactly what you said would happen." My toughest teachers are the ones I still remember. Sure, if you're nice and you're popular the players will like you because you're fun and easy, but that's only a temporary relationship, and it does not survive losing.

Fame and the Worms

One of the things that helped me at Princeton is that I have no desire to be famous, because the Admission Office turns down the guys who would have made me famous. I don't care if I never see my name in the paper. I don't care if I am never on television. I don't care if I don't have to travel 3,000 miles to recruit a big-name player. I don't need any of that to motivate me to do my work. And I know this: No matter where you coached, the worms eat you at the same rate.

■ ■ ■

A Hundred Grand and Nothing

There are kids at Princeton University who, if I were broke, would take up a collection and there would be a hundred grand, right in my pocket. There are kids at Princeton University, if there was some kind of market and I was on sale, they would not give a nickel. That's what happens when you are a fairly uncompromising person. I have never confused understanding with compromise. When you are as direct as I am, you're going to offend some people.

How Players Have Changed

I think the players have changed a little, but not much. Not as much at Princeton as at other places, maybe, because they still have to study, while at other places, not so much—you have to face up to that. But the whole world has changed. The whole world needs more and more understanding—and less compromise. When a player has fifteen other ways to spend his time rather than doing what he should do, the odds against him doing what he should do are greater—that's modern times.

My later Princeton players seemed to have to do more school work than twenty years ago. And they were more focused on getting out and getting good jobs. The Renaissance man has died. I used to tell my players during exam time to practice on their own and almost all of them would. But during the last few years when I'd tell them the same thing, only a few would. I let more guys miss practices, or be late because of papers due, during the last few years than the whole rest of my career.

Still, my friend John McPhee likes to tell the following story about one of my more recent players, Matt Henshon ('91):

"One year, a basketball player submitted an adroitly written and charming essay in application for my spring semester writing course, which would begin on February 1. I picked up the telephone and called Pete. 'One of your basketball players has applied to my course and I'd like to take him, but it's an all-afternoon seminar and I'm not going to take him if he has to get up and leave and go to the gym.'

"In Pete's only tone of voice—his gust-driven toad baritone —he broke in and said, 'What's his name? What's his name?'

" 'Matthew Henshon.'

" 'He can do it. He can do it. What time does your class end?'

" 'Four-twenty.'

" 'He can do it. What's more—let me tell you—if that fucking kid ever walks out early, if he ever misses so much as one minute of your class, he will never play another minute of basketball for Princeton.'

"Matt Henshon became a starter on a championship team."

Premature Retirement

In 1992, after winning four Ivy titles in a row, somehow word started going around that I was considering retirement. I remember telling my coaches, "If I were to retire now, you would hear two statements: First, they would say I won a lot of Ivy titles. Second, I could not win the big one in the NCAA. Now suppose, for the sake of argument, let's say we do not win an Ivy title for four more years and I retire then. You would hear three statements: First, that it was time to get out; second, he had lost the ability to deal with his players; and third, his style of play was no longer functional." In 1995–96, we won the Ivy title and beat UCLA in the tournament and I announced I was retiring. It is easier to say nice things about someone after he has been successful.

Five Hundred and Twenty-Five Wins

It just means I have been around for a while. It's better than 525 losses. A good record just keeps you working. The hardest thing in the world to do is to do one thing particularly well for a long period of time at whatever standards you establish. Take the doctor who delivers his first baby—what a thrill! Does he, thirty years later, get the same thrill? Did Rex Harrison, after a thousand performances of *My Fair Lady*?

You have to realize, you have to know when you've had your day, when it is your time. You must know all that, and there are a lot of signs that show up to indicate it. I look at Kentucky's Rick Pitino and I look at John Calipari and some of these other coaches, and that's the way I used to look and behave. I don't see them or any coaches today sitting on the bench—hardly any of them. They are all standing up. The players today seem to need a more animated coach.

When I look at coaches like Tom Landry, Chuck Noll, and Don Shula, guys who were so great and maybe in later years did not remain so great, I wonder if they didn't get a little tired. I wonder if coaches who are forceful like I am, when they get older, do they see the same things they used to see? I don't compare myself to them in terms of coaching, I just mean in terms of longevity. If you do something well enough you're eventually confronted with the challenge of sustaining your standard of performance over a long period of time. I have done that very well—the same dedication, the same work ethic as when I first started. But in the last couple of years, I've seen a little slipping at the edges, and I've found myself thinking, "Whoa, you're not doing what you're supposed to. You let your assistants do too much coaching, you let little things slide." I found that I wasn't seeing as much on the court. You start thinking this might not be important. And you get tired: Inside yourself, you get the feeling you want to do something that you cannot do any longer. You get tired not only of the game, but of being in the same place for such a long time. A few weeks before I announced my retirement, I told a friend that I used to think the kids felt my coaching was worth five points a game to them. Maybe it was. But I get the sense they do not feel that way now. I think toward the end I was making less of a difference, and that it was time for me to say, Let's turn it over to a younger man.

I think my players on last year's team were terrific kids, and they were getting me at a time when I have less understanding than they need. Today's kids need a lot more understanding. I am just a little bit too rough, a bit too severe for the type of kid who comes to Princeton today. They need support. They don't need somebody like me. I'll always be rooting for these guys and following the box scores wherever I am. They aren't going to miss me—life is like that—and they shouldn't miss me. When you're out the door, it's the next guy's turn.

Now I'm going to try the pro game. Whenever I used to get

a job offer, I would ask myself one question that influenced my decision: What and who could I love? There was and is nothing to love about being a head coach in the pros, not for me. I've had big-figure offers; I couldn't believe anybody would give me that much. But what would I do with the money? Take longer vacations? Drive a Mercedes instead of a Dodge, eat at swanky places, have people wait on me, wear more expensive suits, read the *Wall Street Journal* every day to see how my stocks are doing? What does money mean if you don't love your work?

My job will be as an assistant coach, not as the decision-maker. That's the head coach's job. I'll have some input into the basic decisions, but I won't make the decision. I will work with individuals, give them some advice. That's different from having to tell a guy he is cut. An assistant coach's job is to notice things and try to help the head coach. I know for sure that it will be a different and tough coaching role for me. It's a business. Some guy is making two million dollars, and you have to try to make him better. You have to be like a business-man yourself. It will take a lot of understanding on my part to be able to function. I depend a lot on loyalty between my players and me. But in the pros, you work with a guy and help him get better and two years later he leaves for more money. You see a pro player who has children and is not married, or has been arrested for possessing an illegal gun, or marijuana, or cocaine—you cannot impose your moral standards on him. I'll see how it goes, and if I don't like it I won't stick around. At age sixty-six, I don't think I'll ever have the emotional energy, the patience—all those important things you need—to be a head coach again.

Maybe someday I'll look back on my coaching career and talk about it, but believe me, what I will remember is our basketball family, the personal relationships we've had, and the genuine feelings that will be there forever. I worked hard from the very first day down to the last day. There isn't much difference in my coaching in that respect between the beginning and now. It was always important to me that my players get the best of what I had. It might not have been good, but it was still the best of what I had.

The Final Question

Why did Princeton permit a person like me to coach there for twenty-nine years? They could have found some tall, handsome dude, with the right image. Instead, they had this small guy smoking a cigar and losing his hair. I think they kept me because some of my players seemed to be better people for the experience.

Twenty-Five Little Things to Remember

1. Every little thing counts. If not, why do it?
2. When closely guarded, do not go toward the ball. Go back-door.
3. Whenever you cut, look for a return pass.
4. When you commit to a cut (or back-door) do not stop and do not come back to the ball.
5. Bad shooters are always open.
6. On offense, move the defense.
7. Putting defensive pressure on the ball makes it

harder for the other team to run an offense and gives your team a better chance to defend.

8. In a zone or any defense, when their five men guard your three men, look to throw crosscourt passes.

9. Watch the man in front of you. He shows you what to do.

10. Keep your dribble. Use it when you're going to do something useful.

11. A pass is not a pass when it is made after you've tried to do everything else.

12. A good player knows what he is good at. He also knows what he is not good at and only does the former.

13. You want to be good at those things that happen a lot.

14. When the legs go, the heart and the head follow quickly behind.

15. Defense involves three things: courage, energy, intelligence.

16. If your teammate does not pass the ball to you when you're open and he doesn't say anything, then he did not see you. If he says "I'm sorry," he saw you and did not want to throw you the ball.

17. In trying to learn to do a specific thing, the specific thing is what you must practice. There is little transfer of learning.

18. Whatever you are doing is the most important thing that you're doing while you're doing it.

19. Anyone can be average.

20. Being punctual is good in itself. However, what

is more important is that your punctuality tells your teammates what you think of them.

21. Hardly any players play to lose. Only a few play to win.

22. I like passers. They can see everything.

23. The way you think affects what you see and do.

24. Rarely does a person who competes with his head as well as his body come out second. That was said even before Coach Vince Lombardi by the Greeks and the Romans, and probably by the Chinese.

25. The ability to rebound is in inverse proportion to the distance your house is from the nearest railroad tracks.